You're Only Old Once

You're Only Old Once

Connie Bertelsen Young

You're Only Old Once

Published by
Lighthouse Christian Publishing
SAN 257-4330
5531 Dufferin Drive
Savage, Minnesota, 55378
United States of America

www.lighthousechristianpublishing.com

DEDICATION

This book is dedicated to those who
want to laugh, dance and love through every
stage of life - especially Baby Boomers, Seniors and
those who know that Heaven's gate is closer than ever!

Do not cast me off in the time of old age;
Do not forsake me when my strength fails.
(Psalm 71:9 NKJV)

IN APPRECIATION TO

my best friend and husband, **Dennis Young** *for growing old with me*

Herbert Roebuck, *teacher and author who believes in me*

Bonnie Horg, Darlene Seversen, Pam Shipman, Elaine Loy, *and* **Yvonne Coley,** *for their prayers, for being the special friends they are and encouraging me more than they know.*

Andy Overett *and the professional people at* **Lighthouse Publishing** *for their time and expertise in publishing this book*

Contents

Contents Continued

Introduction

A short time ago, forgetting Mother's reminder, "Life is short," I thought old age seemed far, far away. I took my youth for granted - until it left. Looking back, I realize I was too busy enjoying life to think about the curses of bifocals, wrinkles and gray hair. Rheumatism, laxatives and handicapped parking places weren't a consideration ...then. Admittedly, sometimes I hate being old. And in retrospect, I've realized I've never been content with my age anyway, even as a youngster. That dissatisfaction probably began when I was about three. I wanted to be five so I could go to Kindergarten. I continued to be in a rush to be older throughout my school years, wanting to advance to a particular age so I could do things like go out on a date, drive a car, vote, and so on. But you know, I'm no longer in a hurry.

Like everyone, I began growing old from birth (not to mention the birth of my children, with my ageing particularly advanced at certain stages of their development). Still, I didn't think much about old age until certain tactless people pointed it out to me.

My hairdresser said, "You should color the gray out of your hair. It makes you look old." And then my doctor advised me, "At your age you shouldn't be eating spicy foods." My grandson curiously asked, "What are those little lines on your face, Grandma?" But the worst reminder was when an insensitive saleslady had the nerve to give me her opinion about the beautiful dress I chose. "This is a little young for you. Let's try something else," whereupon she audaciously paraded to a different dress rack, leaving me standing with my elderly mouth wide open. These comments made me think I should go straight to a pharmacy and find a bottle of Geritol.

Well, I'm afraid my age is indeed showing. How often can I repeat, "What did they say?" before they write me off at the club. I can't climb stairs without grunting or remember what I wanted to get between the kitchen and the bedroom, and frankly, I make too many trips to the bathroom.

Those gradual changes in the mirror didn't clue me in - until one day, the reflection was startlingly clear. I was suddenly old enough to get Medicare, discounts at the movies and order from the senior citizen menu at restaurants.

I want to age gracefully, but facing the annoyances of old age influences one's disposition, among other things. I can't seem to move without creaking, stand without swaying and bend without sticking. When I stoop down to pick up something, I look around to see if there's anything else I need to pick up while I'm there. Even getting out of bed in the morning takes a while to get everything moving.

Just like my grandmother did, I now keep a magnifying glass near my reading lamp and a blanket available on my chair. If I sit still very long, I fall asleep. When my husband picks a movie he asks, "Is this the one you want to take a nap with?"

I can't epitomize my life in a few paragraphs but I'll name a few things so you'll understand why I'm so tired.

I've been married twice, have four energetic children, nine genius grandchildren, and countless relatives and friends who know I'm a good cook and have a spare bedroom. Besides the best job of being a homemaker, I've worked as a waitress, a secretary, a teacher, a caregiver, a volunteer, a bookkeeper, a newspaper columnist and a business owner. I've packed and moved 31 times (not including helping my countless relatives and friends to move), planted gardens, prepared meals, hosted parties, baked cookies, washed faces, changed diapers, cleaned toilets, scrubbed, painted, decorated, driven, delivered, scolded, loved, laughed, cried and prayed ... a LOT. And that's just the tip of the iceberg. I'm not just "over the hill," I'm over a mountain.

At this chapter of life, I could use some new eyes so I'll see my wrinkle cream isn't toothpaste, new ears so I can hear the radio without blasting out the neighbors, and new hands that don't tremble when I measure my Metamucil. I'm very glad God promises to make all things new (see Revelation 21:5).

Nevertheless, in this geriatric predicament where I've shockingly found myself, I'm going to try to keep from behaving like a cranky old woman. It's really not so bad if I can share my complaints and laugh. Being cheerful works better than antidepressants. Our ageing is actually slowed down when our hearts are right.

A merry heart does good, like medicine, but a broken spirit dries the bones. (Proverbs 17:22 NKJV)

You've probably heard the saying, "You only live once," or "You're only young once," as an excuse for adventurous living.   As you read <u>You're Only Old</u>

Once, I hope you're encouraged to enjoy life to its fullest adventure and smile along with me. Meanwhile, if you too are noticing the ageing process, be comforted with this wonderful news:

Even to your old age, I am He, And even to gray hairs I will carry you! I have made, and I will bear; Even I will carry, and will deliver you (Isaiah 46:4 NKJV).

Connie Bertelsen Young

1

Fruit Fly in the Night

Being disgusted with the television shows available after *Jeopardy*, I gave up the search, turned the TV off and went to bed a little after 8 p.m. It began cruising my bed about 8:10 as I was already falling into comfortable sleep. I'm not sure exactly what it was, but it had wings. One wouldn't think the tiny thing could make that much noise. Although my hearing isn't what it used to be, the decibel level was outrageous. It could have made *The Guinness Book of Records* as the loudest insect in history.

I tried placing my pillow over my head, hoping it would fly into the kitchen and take a nap on the peaches or something, but the persistent supersonic critter besieged me all night. Few things keep this old woman from getting to sleep but I didn't sleep much that night.

We don't have a cat, but when the sun goes down, the homeless tabbies in my neighborhood gather in our backyard. I counted six felines making the commotion Monday night. The neighbors must think I'm a masochist because when those cats begin their yowling, it sounds like someone's being tortured. But most of the time, I'm surprisingly able to sleep through this noise anyway.

The cats don't bother me as much as the car alarms going off in the middle of the night. Interestingly, nobody ever seems to get up to investigate this deplorable noise. We hear them all over the place during the day too. People ignore them. Actually, their real use isn't to alert the vehicle owner. It's to destroy the burglar's hearing. He'll never be the same. He'll probably retire from auto theft and get into pick-pocketing or something less painful.

Loud snoring doesn't keep me awake. When I was young, two girlfriends shared an apartment with me. They sang in the choir on Sunday mornings, but nothing like the peculiar duet they sang at night while they slept.

My husband's snoring doesn't bother me either. Besides, I remember something a widowed friend of mine said. "Snoring is the sweetest sound this side of Heaven."

There are other things that might disturb one's sleep. Like that horrible rap music that finds a way down my street making my headboard vibrate. And my neighbor's dog barks so much at night that when I hear it during the day, I get sleepy. It's psychological.

Things like dripping faucets, thunderstorms, noisy parties and things going "Bump in the night" bother other people, but not me. However, the tiny noisemaker circling my head kept my eyes wide open, even though I usually sleep soundly. Maybe too soundly. Rigor mortis must begin to set in because I find it extremely difficult to revive in the morning. My grandkids gave me a lovely flannel nightgown with a warning on it. "Just because I'm up doesn't mean I'm awake." They know I resurrect slowly. And they know what I believe about those weird morning persons.

"He who blesses his friend with a loud voice, rising early in the morning, It will be counted a curse to him" (Proverbs 27:14 NKJV).

That miniature dive bomber's flight plan kept me tossing and turning all night, causing more cursing than blessing, and the bedroom was an unholy mess by morning. At intervals, I used my pillow to try to smash the little kamikaze, but the only thing that got smashed was the lamp.

After the sun came up and the alarm clock from Hell rang, and after, due to lack of sleep and diminishing eyesight, I blindly reached for the salt and peppered the oatmeal while it cooked.

I determined to do something about the pest problem. I bought one of those bug bomb things filling the room with insecticide. Well, I think I killed the carpet.

2

Memories of Curbside Collection

Do not say, "Why were the former days better than these?" For you do not inquire wisely concerning this (Ecclesiastes 7:10 NKJV).

We senior citizens reminisce about the good old days, but although I may recollect the earlier years with fondness, I know... some things weren't so good. I'm thankful for modern conveniences, one of which I was thinking about today.

I went outdoors to wash the kitchen window before the weather changed. (You know one can usually count on a storm when windows are washed.) But I found myself daydreaming instead of washing the window, and I sat in the sunshine and watched and listened to our city's monstrous garbage trucks, squealing down the block.

The great thing about retirement is there's time to smell the flowers - although, actually it wasn't flowers I smelled this time.

Starting and stopping with brakes squeaking, the enormous trucks noisily groaned, mechanically lifting and dumping garbage containers into the back. Then they return the containers to the curb, compact the rubbish and move a little space down the road.

I remember the old, heavy, galvanized steel garbage cans that sat in our back yard behind a fence (where garbage cans ought to be). They were weighty when full and hard to lift. But the huge plastic bins we have now can fairly easily be rolled to the curb. They're a lot different than the cans which used to line the residential sidewalks of America on trash day.

Various colors, shapes and sizes of garbage cans, boxes, and junk blemished the streets. Block after block of unsightly containers leaning against one another, always a few cans turned over with the owner's private rubbish exposed to the eyes of the world. The cans were usually bent and twisted because it looked like the garbage men (called sanitation workers now) used them to take out their inner anxieties. With brute strength they lifted those containers and tipped them into the dump truck. Still, they didn't complain about an extra barrel or two. If you put the box the washing machine came in, a broken bicycle or the terminated Christmas tree, they disposed of it all without a fuss – and without a generic warning note in red saying, "These items cannot be disposed until cut in small pieces and placed in the correct container." In fact, in 1951 my dad lost a perfectly good push mower by parking it too close to the pickup area.

Those old garbage cans were an irresistible source of delight to the neighborhood dogs and cats. They toppled them over during their attempts to get at the discarded tuna surprise or whatever, strewing a shocking number of beer cans down the block.

5

The new containers are pretty much canine-proof and cans go in the recycle bin.

Everyone's involved in recycling and it's easy to get cash for aluminum cans. Throwing cans out the window of a vehicle used to only be done by a litterbug; now only a philanthropist will do it. Just throw out an empty can in certain neighborhoods and you'll see some incredible gymnastics. There are fewer cans in the bin if it sits at the curb very long before collection too.

Before the country finally figured out the wisdom of recycling, my mother understood it perfectly. She recycled everything from gift wrap to peanut butter jars. Many things were used over and over. The coffee grounds, egg shells and vegetable peelings were collected for compost. The wash water watered the garden.

Clothes were recycled by us and all our relatives. I wore my cousin's hand-me-downs after my sister grew out of them. Then they were used again by those younger than me. If nobody was left to fit them and they weren't threadbare after passing them around, they went to the Salvation Army... that is, if mother couldn't use the buttons or the zippers for making something else. And of course the scraps of material could often be used for making quilts.

What was left from meals after we ate was warmed up another night, instead of being dumped into a garbage disposal. In fact, we were pretty much guaranteed of having leftovers on Friday night if there was even a little food remaining to be put back in the icebox after our meals.

Mom didn't need a garbage can that held much - she barely filled a small one. Besides, we had a dog.

Our dog helped with the "Waste not - want not" business too. She waited for treats beneath the table and with any luck would assist in the disappearance of the vegetables for which I was not particularly fond. So I occasionally had a little help producing a clean plate, which was mandatory before desert. Anyway, one rarely found food items in the garbage. But it's different now.

Somebody decided we need three enormous bins for everything that's thrown out nowadays because few people have the mentality my parents had. But my parents weren't lazy. They knew what the Bible had to say about that:

He who is slothful in his work is a brother to him who is a great destroyer (Proverbs 18:9 NKJV).

With that in mind, I decided I'd better get busy and clean my kitchen window. I don't see any clouds in the sky... yet. Meanwhile, although I appreciate these big garbage bins, I wonder if we're throwing away too much. Homeless people seem to think so.

3

The Health Food Store

Years ago, when health food products began appearing faster than frozen turkeys in November, I bought my share of Ginseng, drank carrot juice and read Adele Davis' books. Over the years I lost my appetite for nutritional concoctions prepared in the blender, avoided recipes with tofu and became careless, indulging in too much salt, sugar and junk food. It has been awhile since brewer's yeast, wheat germ and sprouts were on my grocery list, but I've decided I better be more conscientious about what goes on this senior citizen's plate. So, with good intentions, I made a trip to the health food store.

It's an eye-opening experience to rediscover the health food store. It's not what it used to be. I never dreamed of what's being offered there and I can see I've neglected a marvelous resource. I was inspired to find row after row of health promises appearing on bottles of vitamins, herbal assortments and miracle pills. The mere product names gave me hope.

Consider the joy I felt when finding a bottle of *Slim and Firm.* I always knew there had to be an alternative to aerobic exercise. Elated, I grabbed bottles from the shelf with delightful names like *Fat Fighter* and *Veggie Max*.

Supposedly, *Veggie Max is* a supplement to satisfy all one's vegetable needs. I like vegetables now, but if that had been available when I was a kid, I would have been excused from the table a lot sooner. One gulp and it would have been over. Instead, I lost at least a year of my life at the dinner table between the ages of three and twelve. My parents believed in Daniel's approach to eating. (See Daniel 1:11-16).

Although I didn't want to dismiss the magnificent possibilities the products offered, I had to wonder. With so many impressive diet helps available, there were certainly a large number of overweight people in the store. As I looked around, another shelf of goodies caught my eye.

My heart beat faster when I saw the bold letters *"Anti-Aging"* on a plastic bottle filled with a mysterious beet colored liquid. (Now, they can't sell this stuff with those promises unless it's proven to work ...right?) It was next to the cod liver oil and the *Happy Camper* drink. I knew the inevitable consequences of cod liver oil, but I wasn't sure what the *Happy Camper* drink could do; nevertheless, I thought of donating a bottle or two to a couple of DMV employees, even if the alcohol content seemed a bit high.

Well, eventually I found out I was disillusioned by labels. For instance, I hoped the *Buzz Off* spray might work when certain groups of door-to-door people appeared - but I should have known it's for repelling insects. And too bad *Sun-Lights* won't dispel fog. It's only a hair lightener. But my hair is plenty light and I'm afraid I'm getting a bald spot.

Still, there are preventatives, cures and remedies worth a try. I think. They're a little pricey, but I'll save some money if I don't have to buy new clothes - that is, if the bottle of *Slim and Firm* does what it says. Then I'll fit the smaller sizes I've kept in my closet for many years (in case I lose weight). Of course, this is all depending upon whether I can remove this darn child-proof cap.

4

A Real American Hero

There is no remembrance of former things, nor will there be any remembrance of things that are to come by those who will come after (Ecclesiastes 1:11 NKJV).

Perhaps someday my great, great, grandchildren will read this book and get some picture of how different our lives were from theirs. The world in which my great grandparents lived has made enormous changes, and due to ever-expanding technology, we see things changing at an even more rapid pace today.

For instance, we can easily find almost anything we want on the internet. The newspaper is one example, so I think having newspaper boys will become a thing of the past. They've almost disappeared already.

I've observed a lot of paper boys over the years. They had certain characteristics in common, although they came in various shapes and colors. Riding a bicycle with a newspaper holder of some sort, they *always* peeled out on my driveway. Generally, he was one of the most ambitious young men on the block. (My current delivery person is a woman who uses a vehicle, but she *still* peels out on my driveway.)

Curiously, an idiosyncrasy they shared, was an inability to hit the front porch. One rarely found the news in this obvious place. Eventually, the unique deliverer designated his preference, like on top of the rare bonsai for which I paid the nurseryman forty dollars when it was a mere twig. But I felt fortunate when the paper made it to the flower bed. Sometimes it landed so far from the porch, on a foggy day, I couldn't find it.

Remember the cartoon with Fred Flintstone's disgruntlement depicted in his relationship with Arnold? It was a comical stereotype representing many household's vexation with the paper boy, but the truth is, those newspaper carriers were misunderstood.

The kid didn't intentionally fling the paper on the roof. He was merely trying to toss it through the basketball hoop. And of course he didn't mean to deliver it late. His bicycle got a flat in front of the arcade.

Having a paper route wasn't an easy job. It required facing mean dogs, careless drivers and people who wouldn't tip. Rain or storm, the carrier got out of bed before the sun came up and began his job to deliver the news while it was still dark. Well, sometimes.

Those paper boys were unique entities. Who knows how long we'll have the pleasure of having a newspaper delivered this way to our homes? So I just wanted to show my appreciation to the individuals who have delivered my newspapers to my front porch – or at least the general vicinity.

5

Interior Decorating

Making a house a home has been one of my most favorite things to do. I was fortunate to have been a homemaker while my children were small and for many years. But there isn't much pride in this humble title anymore. It's a rarity to find women who don't have jobs or careers outside of the home. Anyway, I hope I'm not stoned by those ambitious young women who are forced to work, or who prefer the workplace, but the truth is, I've always loved housework, especially when it came to interior decorating.

Gayle, my pastor's wife, who visited many households over the years, taught me something she usually found true based on the looks of a home. She believes there's a correlation between the appearance of one's residence and an individual's spiritual condition and personality.

Mother always said, "Cleanliness is next to Godliness," so I've always tried to keep things pretty clean. But I was a little concerned, wondering what my home expressed to Gayle. Then I happened to hear a home and garden show make it clear. I learned my style is "shabby-chic" which pretty much says it all.

"Shabby-chic" is the *dernier cri* in decorating, combining elegant things like precious silver, crystal vases, dainty embroidery and pretty things with weathered pieces, flea market finds, funky collections, antiques and less-than-perfect items. That's me alright, especially the antique and less-than-perfect part. Indeed, there is a correlation with my home decorating and me. I believe God is making me into the ultimate design that He wants me to be. Meanwhile, until I get the complete makeover, (see 1 John 3:2) you could say I'm a shabby-chic bedizenment.

It's pretty cool that the way I've always decorated became the rage. "Shabby-chic" has been my style since I was eighteen. Mother gave me a few items for my first independent residence and I combined them with other meager possessions in my apartment. Back then, posters, old bottles and plastic daisies were assimilated with the lace doilies, mismatched silver and china pieces. *Voila!* It was "shabby-chic."

I'm afraid this style gives my husband an excuse for keeping his dilapidated recliner - even though that chair was never chic and surpassed shabby years ago. Anyway, it remains and continues to be abused and battered by grandkids who love to change the positions with the lever and climb on it to get to Grandpa's lap. Well, that old chair doesn't represent my style; however, something can be said for the correlation between it and my husband's personality, but that's all I'm going to say about that. Anyway, one's home and favorite things definitely represent something, so I've paid more attention to the way my friends decorate. One can tell quite a lot about a person that way. And if you look closely, you'll find things about their spiritual condition and priorities concerning God, family and friends. Above all, you'll find evidence of what the homeowner loves.

In small ways, our homes and possessions show whether we're careless, perfectionistic, artistic, musical, hospitable, organized, intellectual, fun, flexible, joyful or depressed among other things. Many signs can be found. If the owners like to cook, you'll notice that fact by checking out the kitchen. If they're athletic, prefer gardening, or have creative inclinations, you'll see the tools somewhere. You can probably find out something about the owner's health if you see what's in the pantry or refrigerator. Even couch potatoes leave their mark on a home. What's on the computer, movie collections, and favorite books will shout one's character.

My friend Gayle said it takes more than a onetime surveillance before you can make an appreciative observation. Of course, only God knows a person completely so we mustn't judge. But it's a good thing to take time to see people for who they are with acceptance and love.

I'm convinced that interior decorating is more revealing than most of us realize. But at this point I'm not talking about the visible stuff that moth and rust destroy and where thieves can break in and steal. I'm thinking of the interior of the heart.

Create in me a clean heart, O God, And renew a steadfast spirit within me (Psalm 51:10 NKJV).

6

Sadie Dog

*A righteous man regards the life of his animal,
But the tender mercies of the wicked are cruel*
(Proverbs 12:10 NKJV).

Our dog, Sadie, came to live with us a few years
ago when our rancher friend needed to find a home
for her. A busy man, tending to livestock and ranch
work, he didn't have time to give her the attention he
felt she deserved.

Sadie, a smart Queensland/Aussie mix, wanted
companionship and loved to play, so in her
loneliness she had turned to horses for community.
She even developed an uncanny, bouncy pony
prance, incredibly resembling the movement of the
horses as she raced with them. Unfortunately, it
wasn't long before the horses made it clear they
didn't want a pup in their social circle. I supposed
she resented their rejection, and about that same

time, she began grabbing their tails and hanging on and swinging, a sorry yet hilarious sight to see.

Our friend didn't have time to train her, and he didn't have the heart to keep her tied up, so he asked us if we wanted her. We had some acreage for her to run, and with enthusiasm, she soon adjusted to chasing squirrels and lizards instead of horses.

We've grown to appreciate Sadie. She has qualities I'd like to see in the human race. For instance, her affection for me is obvious. I wish I was so well-liked by people. And frankly, sometimes I wish I liked people so much. Of course, humans can't wag a tail when they're glad to see each other, but it would be nice if they showed more delight.

I never have doubts about what my dog's thinking. It's about food. But there's no need to spend hours in the kitchen to impress her with the cuisine. She's not a picky eater and she's never had a problem with leftovers or failed recipes.

Sadie respects me, stopping whatever she's doing when I call. She doesn't mind whether or not I've done my hair, my housework, or if I feel like talking – she still thinks I'm wonderful. And unlike humans who don't understand, communication with her is uncomplicated. She responds wonderfully to certain words. It's a small and simple vocabulary, but it's tough making people comprehend the same ones.

For example, although it's one of the first words a human speaks, there are people who just don't get the word, "No." Although Sadie understands it, I've learned that using this word is a waste of time with certain individuals. Telephone solicitors and door-to-door salesmen rarely get it; unlike Sadie's quick response to the word, I'm forced to hang up the phone while they're talking or shut the door in their face. And parents would get a break if their children could be taught to be as responsive as Sadie is to "No." Not to mention the most useful command, "Sit."

Human acknowledgement of those words would certainly make things easier for teachers too. Funny, our youth pick up slang easy enough. Why is this basic dog lingo so hard to teach to people?

If I throw a ball or stick and tell Sadie to "Get it," she immediately races for it. But I'm afraid even my husband is bewildered by rudimentary dog vernacular. He especially has this problem when we go shopping at the local department stores. If I suggest for him I want to "Get it," I've noticed delayed response and recurrent cognitive losses.

I wish people, young and old, would understand the importance of the simple commands my pooch knows. I think it would eliminate a lot of stress in the world.

"It's okay," is the phrase that I tell Sadie when something disturbs her. It gives comfort to her. If only people would say this to each other more. And as a matter of fact, an occasional pat on the back, like I give to Sadie, wouldn't hurt either!

7
Where are the Good Guys?

I'm weary of the media's repetitive reporting whenever there's a crime committed, especially the more notorious ones. Why is it that the more shocking or wicked the offense is, the more likely the exposure? It seems to me that the bad guy gets way too much attention.

Those kind of depressing press releases seem to grow in sensationalism. Criminal misdeeds are publicized over and over again, appearing in headlines and pictures on television and in the newspaper. Murderers and thieves become a little too familiar to everyone. Shamefully, their photographs are recognized quicker than those of people who have helped our society through admirable accomplishments.

Unfortunately, sensationalism has always appealed to the young, and youth tend to imitate what is popular. Sadly, we see too many copycat crimes. Perhaps this is because there are those who can no longer differentiate between the hero and the scoundrel.

It's clear that a generation of people are unaware of what is truly good, and they are deceived and desensitized to what is evil. One reason for this is because of the entertainment industry. Extraordinary actors excite their audience while they are highlighted in unscrupulous, brutal and startling scenes. Villains are glorified in movies.

Being entertained has a high place in our society, and because of the lust for entertainment, millions of viewers are unwittingly beckoned into a place of darkness, exchanging wholesomeness and truth. Regular exposure to decadence seems to cause people to lose discernment and they become impressed with those who behave wickedly, not perceiving the reality.

Woe to those who call evil good, and good evil; Who put darkness for light, and light for darkness; Who put bitter for sweet, and sweet for bitter! (Isaiah 5:20 NKJV)

For many, being politically correct is more important than recognizing sin as sin. Besides, political correctness as defined by the world absolutely doesn't fit with God's Word.

I can hear my grandchildren laughing at me, but I remember the good guys in shows like *The Lone Ranger, Father Knows Best* and *Highway Patrol.* And I've noticed classic enduring stories such as *Peter Pan, Superman* and *Cinderella* are reproduced nowadays with crass dialogue and worldly scenes. *Snow White* isn't so "white" anymore. Producers have exchanged purity for sex, violence and blaspheming.

Yes, my idea of good entertainment is old-fashioned. I don't want everything to go back to the way it was, but I maintain that right and wrong is clearly defined by God.

Along with other things, trends, fashion, and the selfish desire for gratification has destroyed the image of the good guy on the white horse that we used to see. His pure simplicity seems to have been lost in a world of sensationalism. So where are the good guys?

I want to see the good guys. But meanwhile, we need to see the good guys in our mirrors. But the fact is, we can only really be "good guys" through Jesus Christ. He is the greatest example of integrity and the only perfect role model to imitate.

For I have given you an example, that you should do as I have done to you (John 13:15 NKJV).

8

Of Checks and Balances

As a child, I watched my dad going over the household bills as he sat at a huge oak desk with built-in file slots and deep drawers. The room emanated a distinctive leathery smell mixed with tobacco. I remember items sitting on the desktop that you don't see much anymore.

A small Success calendar with metal rings for refilling each year, an old black telephone with a smooth cord and a circular dial in the center, a Lucky Strike ashtray, a 2-ounce bottle of Schaeffer Script Ink and a 1936 Royal portable typewriter sat on his desk among other things.

I learned to type on that old typewriter, and I loved filling a fountain pen from the ink jar and printing my name – even if it seemed impossible to keep telltale stains of ink from my fingers.

A new adding machine with a stream of skinny paper was added to the desk by the time I graduated from high school, but Dad never had a hand held calculator or a computer. I remember his huge black, business checkbook too. It was almost as big as a stack of two or three *Saturday Evening Post* magazines. The checks were a unique gold color with distinctive thin lines and black calligraphy, indicating places for the details of the check to be written.

For those that still use them, checks have everything imaginable printed on them nowadays. I suppose it's a matter of personal taste but I never wanted to make the house payment with a picture of Mickey Mouse on the check. There was something frivolous about sending more than a quarter of our income off with a cartoon character.

Checks used to be free. The bank supplied them for Dad, but now they sell them. They want to encourage automated payment so they don't have to pay employees. Even though I know I'll be forced to change, I like touching something when I'm paying a bill. My money disappears fast enough.

I didn't use to have trouble using checks for payment anywhere. Once by mistake, I accidentally wrote a check to Sears and Roebuck when I purchased a blouse at Montgomery Wards. The bank still took it and it didn't matter a bit that the blouse I bought shrunk when I washed it.

I thought it was funny when they used to ask, "Is this information correct?" Why ask? If I were dishonest, I wouldn't say, "No, that's not my name and address." Some stores won't take checks anymore. Since scanning the check or checking for identification hasn't stopped the criminal, they've started scanning people. The Bible predicted something about that in Revelation 13:18. I'm annoyed when I find checks in my mailbox sent by a bank or credit card company. My name and address are on them and they encourage me to use them for whatever my heart desires - with tempting suggestions included. Trouble is, my husband says they give me more "cash available" than he can afford. He leans towards thinking we should keep our cash available at home instead of in an account where they charge us for using our money. Actually, all of it could fit in a Mason jar anyway.

I suppose checks will be disappearing soon because of computerized bill paying and banking nowadays. Someday the grandkids will find antique value in our checks and frame them and hang them on their walls as a conversation piece. Maybe they'll be hanging up ink pens in vintage displays also.

9

Of Weddings and Marriages

Sadly, an incredible number of marriages end in divorce. You'd think this fact in itself should be enough to slow down applications for marriage licenses. But besides the alarming divorce rate, there's something else I find disturbing. It's many of the weddings nowadays.

Let me be clear. It isn't just because I don't appreciate pretentious receptions, lengthy ceremonies, exorbitantly priced bridal gowns, flashy wedding rings, extravagant invitations and gaudy decorations. If couples want to spend thousands of dollars on these items when children are starving to death in other parts of the world, that's their choice. Of course they could make a down payment on a house or pay off their credit cards instead of opting to be the center of attention for a couple hours.

But no, I'm not unhappy about weddings just because the couple could better use the money they're squandering. (I won't even begin my tirade concerning same sex weddings here because the Bible clearly makes no bones about it. See Romans 1:26-28 if there is any doubt.)

Please understand that I believe in righteous marriage. But let me explain why I'm disturbed by weddings. It's when people are obsessed with them - when women in particular are more interested in being a bride than being a wife.

Sometimes people need to have a second chance, but second and third weddings are too common, and they may be happening because the knot was tied too loose.

Weddings are supposed to be a holy ceremony for the couple who love each other and determine to remain together for the rest of their lives, no matter what! But some obviously don't trust their mate enough to count on the promise made at the altar anyway, with prenuptial agreements giving evidence to that fact.

Consider the weddings of the past. There was a time when two young people met and fell in love followed by an engagement period before that special day when the vows, "Until death do us part" were solemnly spoken. When the groom kissed the bride, he didn't swallow her face, and they probably hadn't practiced kissing too much yet anyway.

Nowadays, couples are standing at the altar before they know what they want to be when they grow up. They haven't been together long enough to know what kind of credit card bill their future mate has established, and the ceremonial kiss is a marathon event – with not much doubt about other particulars partaken ahead of time.

I heard a bride-to-be express concern about whether it was proper to have a sheet cake instead of a tier cake. If she were really conscientious about what's correct, she wouldn't have been pregnant; yet she still wore a white gown.

I'd like to know, what gift do you buy for a bride who already had a wedding? You know she already has a toaster. I'm irked when a woman puts her name on the bride registries more than once. Even the first time seems audacious to me. I never liked the idea of being told what gift I should give.

Alas. I guess a psychiatrist might tell me there's a reason why I look at it all so critically. It might be because I blew it myself. Many years ago I experienced the devastating mutilation of divorce. And I can't rationalize away the blame. It takes two.

The divorce rate was at an all-time high when those of us who are now seniors were younger. Of course, there are plenty couples who don't bother to get married, so that may be the reason the statistics are lower.

We can pray that the future generation will get it right. Most married people know it takes a miracle for two human beings to live together without killing each other. Good marriages take three. Without the love of God, no couple will be fully satisfied and find true happiness.

I'm thankful that God gave me a second chance for a happy marriage. And just for the record, we had a private ceremony and stated our vows in church with only our pastor and two witnesses attending. It wasn't fancy and there was no reception, even though I certainly could have used a new toaster.

10

Remembering What I Forgot

I can't remember who said, "You have to use your memory in order to keep it," but it's true. If we don't use it, we will lose it.

Poor memory is a frequent complaint among senior citizens; nevertheless, this shouldn't be attributed to old age. The real problem has to do with lack of use. We need to be concerned when our brains are underused. That's the difficulty with retirement...for some.

So since the brain functions best with use, why do people keep telling me, "Connie, you think too much!" Is that possible? I want to do what I can to avoid senility and forgetfulness. Of course, I don't suppose anyone really has "total recall" (except my X).

I find it upsetting when I draw a blank about things I should remember. Besides, the human brain has as many as 500 trillion synaptic connections which drive emotions, create thoughts and behaviors. Surely there's enough power there to help me remember where I left my eyeglasses.

God has given us an incredibly huge potential to think, feel, learn and create. It's our responsibility to use what He has given us.

I will praise You, for I am fearfully and wonderfully made; Marvelous are Your works, And that my soul knows very well (Psalm 139 NKJV).

My memory problem might be a matter of prioritizing since I tend to get too many irons in the fire; so, I made a list of priorities of what I should be doing. Now... (you know what I'm going to say next), if only I could remember where I put the list.

Actually, it's little things I forget, not the big stuff. Things like wondering if I already took my vitamin, trying to remember what I was looking for in the storeroom, and if I watered the house plants. I've been a block or two away from home and wonder if I remembered to turn off the coffee maker.

Besides writing the wrong year on my checks, I have a peculiar problem with numbers. At the mall, I never remember how many pairs of shoes are already in my closet. I forget how much I weigh when someone offers dessert. And I'm at a loss for words when someone asks how old I am. I forget that my peers are no older than me ... until I see the photos.

Despite my memory problems, there are some things I'd like to forget. I'd like to forget that I sent a Christmas card to my Aunt Rita and Uncle George. Well, my Uncle had died three years earlier. Fortunately, my elderly aunt was gracious about it. She was thrilled that I thought Uncle George was still with her – no one else understood why she talked with him every day.

Children innocently say, "I forgot" when they don't know the answer. I've been saying that quite a bit lately. I guess there is a second childhood. I think I'm there. And I'd really love to go outside and play.

11

One Ringy Dingy

The telephone has come a long way since it was invented in 1876. I still have a rather old telephone hanging on my wall in the kitchen. One day my grandson asked, "What's that?"

I have a cellular phone too, but even that's an antique, according to my granddaughter, who along with a few earrings, appears to have a phone permanently planted to her left ear.

Phone use took a major turn in the 1920's when candlestick phones were used for social interaction, especially among women. The lines were tied up further by the 1950's when it became a trend for teenagers to socialize via Ma Bell.

I remember rushing to pick up the phone on the first ring when I was a teen. I certainly didn't want my friends to ever think our home had a phone shortage, even if we did only have one.

Most residents in our small community had party lines when I was a kid. My friends and I kept a good account of what was going on around us in those days. Mother made us hang up when she caught us, but not before we got to know our neighbors better.

We learned phones could be used to do a lot of things. We let our "fingers do the walking" by doing things like ordering pizza, dialing the time or dialing a prayer. Desperate people could even dial a date. Nowadays, phones can do a lot more than that and everyone has a private line. Maybe.

Phones have changed the quality of life. Some calls are done by computer, and with Skype you can see the caller and they can see you. But I have to tell you, this bothers me. I'm not always available for viewing when the phone rings. And to the amazement of my grandkids, I don't always answer the phone.

In the early sixties, the answering machine was a godsend to those of us who wanted to live in peace, or just wanted our ears to heal. Telemarketing, which we've all come to know and hate used to interrupt dinner. My husband put a message on our answering machine that said, "Please reach out and touch someone else, we're busy!" Phone etiquette has never been his best gift.

People who dial the wrong number are particularly annoying to him. After several weeks of our phone ringing day and night with someone asking for "Bobby," my husband answered the phone with the intention of stopping the irritating calls. When the caller asked, "Is Bobby there?" He gloomily responded, "I'm sorry. Bobby died." So if your name is Bobby, you may want to call home.

Amazingly, our new phone informs us of who is calling. Supposedly. But whoever that lady is announcing the caller certainly has trouble with pronunciations. It happens a lot. I was concerned the day I thought she said it was the IRS, but I knew that bogus calls were being made by people pretending to represent them. But it was my friend, Iris, not the IRS.

People are eliminating their house phones and using cell phones for everything, so I see another item which will be in our memories of bygone days. Then the only excuse I'll have for not answering my phone is forgetting to have it with me. And the way things are moving, they'll probably figure out a way to make the phone an implant. Maybe they have already. I've never see my granddaughter without it.

Alexander Graham Bell, you didn't know what you started. I think the telephone should be on the list of inventions that have changed our lives the most.

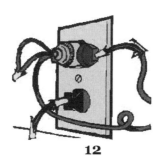

12

Information Overload

My baby boomer brain is inundated with 21st century data. (Not to mention 20th century stuff that I haven't caught up with yet.) I feel bombarded with massive stimuluses' and forced to cogitate enormous amounts of information just to survive on this planet.

There are countless choices in every imaginable product from soup to nuts. I can't order a cup of coffee without selecting from a ridiculously long list. I get overwhelmed with the myriad of options for things like insurance, health care, and various organizations. And I also must pick from an incredible number of gas stations, grocery stores and churches. There are hundreds of channels on my television - which are really unnecessary since I rarely tune in to more than a couple of them. Then there are PCs laptops, desktops, iPads, and all the other stuff I don't own and know the name of yet.

All that high tech paraphernalia is the toughest for me to figure out and sort through. Even though I do my best to keep up, I find it embarrassing when I "don't get it." I want to learn and grow and change like my pastor says I must, but at my age, I don't know where to begin. I feel unequipped ... and admittedly, a little uninspired.

Although once resistant to entering cyberspace, I finally surrendered. I remember not comprehending Mother's resistance to what she called "complicated" and "pointless" things like automatic dishwashers when they first came out. Now I understand. And with the great leaps made in technology, things are changing at a faster pace in my lifetime than it did in hers.

As it is, the computer I bought a mere three years ago is already outdated and problematic. I think they're built with a "time bomb" in them. Coffee makers are like that too. They don't last long before they crash. It isn't just the cost of replacement that distresses me. It's figuring out which one to select from so many choices - and then figuring out how to make the device, with so many switches and parts, run.

I like simplicity. I kept my old drip coffee pot from the fifties. I don't mind boiling water. Young people don't want that experience unless they have a special appliance to do it for them. And I find it odd that some can operate that complex stuff, but those same prodigies can't cook from a recipe.

I'm a good cook, but learning how to use a computer and the Internet was an enormous task. The World Wide Web makes me crazy. I have a hard enough time keeping up with my neighbors.

"Having it all" is a lot to process. But is there anything you can't find by Googling it? Nevertheless, real life can't be found online.

Social media may offer thousands to one's "friends" list without human contact. But I'd rather share a cup of coffee with one dear friend than use a mouse to interact with unlimited people any day. Tweeting should only be the sounds birds make, and I don't believe I can really have much relationship with 900 million people on Facebook.

Someone said the WWW is similar to a spider's web that captures an insect and sucks the life out of it. And many of us have been "caught" on the Web, especially if we have too much time on our hands. One thing leads to another. Are there rehabilitation programs to get detoxed after spending too much time there?

I admit I don't have the appreciation or the savvy my grandchildren have. They're comfortable racing on the digital highway. But I don't text with them because I can't figure out their abbreviations, I don't play those masochistically games and I don't wear ear buds. I'll be getting a hearing aid soon enough.

The Bible indicates fools hate knowledge (Proverbs 1:22), but not everyone is cut out to enjoy all the stuff that entices technophile personalities. Email is enough. Sometimes it's too much.

I went on a short vacation recently. Upon return, I found 29 pieces of email waiting for me. My Philodendron grew half an inch while I was downloading. The email contained photographs, jokes, bogus reports, prayer requests, virus warnings, get rich schemes and a good luck letter.

The good luck letter allegedly became a curse if the recipient deleted it. I felt like doing some cursing myself after all the time I wasted. But I smiled when I saw, "Find your perfect mate" in my inbox. Just for fun, I checked out the options while my husband was napping.

With so much nonsense shooting through cyberspace, I automatically delete most things forwarded. I don't fall for words like "This is so cute" or "Important information."

People once said computers will simplify our lives. We know better now. I remember the simpler day before computers. I'd reach inside my mailbox (out by the street) to get my mail. In those days, I wasn't worried that my mail contained a virus unless the mailman was sick. I enjoyed receiving handwritten letters from people in those days. Now, fewer people know how to use an ink pen.

"This world is not my home," the old song says. I'm glad about that. I get lost in this one.

13

Time for an Invisible Break

I had a bad-hair day...all week, yet I've always said, a bad-heart day is worse. But ashamedly, it does seem like one can instigate the other for me.

Why is it when I'm in a bad mood or lounging in my bath robe, I run out of something so I need to go to the store? And it never fails, when I'm there I run into people who want to talk or insist on doing lunch. But all I want to do is go home and hide under a blanket.

Sometimes I want to be invisible. If I could snap my fingers and disappear for a while, I'd do it. I'd avoid a lot of uncomfortable situations.

For sure I'd like to be invisible when I first get out of bed in the morning. And once in a while it would be nice to be unseen when somebody needs another volunteer. I'm thinking it would be good to be invisible when my husband finds the bill for our charge account that came in the mail today.

If nobody could see me, I'd order those drippy sauce covered ribs that leave a mess on my face when we go out to eat. I might even run a red light instead of waiting so long in an intersection where no cars are visible for miles.

The humiliation I've experienced in previous shopping experiences could have been avoided if only I'd been invisible. Like the day at the grocery store when I accidentally banged my shopping cart into the person holding several cartons of eggs. And another time when the produce guy glared at me for putting back the banana I tore from a bunch after I inspected it.

Last Wednesday the checker advised me that my purchase was $20.37. From the depth of my purse I had already produced eighteen ones, two quarters, four dimes, two nickels and twenty-four pennies on the counter – and I was still short. I wanted to disappear.

I've even wanted to be invisible at church. Like when I had to blow my nose and I only had a pair of socks in my purse, or at the potluck when I found a hair in the salad (and I'm the one who made the salad). Then there was the time when a long piece of toilet paper stuck to my shoe and followed me to the front pew.

If I *were* invisible I'd find out what's *really* going on in the Oval Office, I'd wear a swimsuit to public beaches, and I'd find out what my sister-in-law puts in her potato salad. I wouldn't always answer the doorbell (even though I'll always wonder if it was the Publishers Clearing House the last time I failed to answer).

I could find out for sure what that charity organization is really doing with our contributions. I'd watch to see how the guy with the sign strapped to his back that says, "Please help me buy food for my children" uses donations.

I can think of a lot of places where it would be fun to be a "mouse in the corner" and listen in. But I suppose I wouldn't like to hear everything that's said behind my back. Some things are bad enough when they're said to my face.

Today was one of those days I wanted to vanish from the human race, so I took a nap, hoping that a little rest would cheer me up. When my husband came home he asked, "What are you doing under that blanket in the middle of the afternoon?"

"Being invisible," I sighed.

Funny, the next thing he said was, "Did the mail come?"

Sometimes I need to hide and get away from it all, but only Angels can be invisible. And the fact is, social engagement is necessary for human health - and even longevity. There is ample evidence that social isolation is a risk factor for early mortality. The Bible advises against it.

Not forsaking the assembling of ourselves together, as is the manner of some, but exhorting one another, and so much more as you see the Day approaching (Hebrews 10:25 NKJV).

14

Wrinkles Are Beautiful

I have to admit, commercials used to have a profound effect on my life. Because of my exposure, I bought those stupid slicers and dicers, ordered a lot of pizza and colored my hair. A little blue butterfly flipping across the screen made me think I needed sleep, and in flash, another ad made me think I needed to wake up and get one of those amazing exercise machines.

Advertisements can be convincing, producing fallacious beliefs in people. Sometimes it's a subliminal message. I don't know about you, but thoughts such as my teeth, my collars and my toilet need whitening will be with me forever. They try to make us believe *anywhere* we can possibly squirt a product smells badly. And the compelling notion, "You need to go shopping," robs us of the contentment that the Apostle Paul showed in Philippians 4:11-12. (Of course, he didn't have television.)

The commercials that get my goat lately are the ones trying to convince us that wrinkles are unacceptable. If that's true, I'm in trouble! But it's not true. They want us to believe "wrinkle" is a dirty seven letter word. But I can't let them sell me that package.

Wrinkles don't mean life is over. Consider the raisin. Even the grape has a second career. And aging is not the enemy, although we're continually offered "weapons" to fight it. The "experts" advise us to apply slippery, smelly and expensive applications to our skin. There are moisturizers, renewal treatments, creams and diffusers, with Botox and plastic surgery for the very rich and wrinkled. They tell us to avoid sunshine, never squint or frown and always sleep on our backs to keep our skin from hanging the wrong direction. Well, it's too late - and that's all I'm going to say about that.

Millions of dollars are spent to fight the inevitable. But the skin covering our bones will wrinkle and sag sooner or later, no matter what anti-wrinkle product or method people refinance their houses to buy.

I see those lines as something that give character, earned through life experience. I maintain that crow's feet are prestigious marks of baby boomers.

The creases between my eyebrows were earned from raising teenagers. The little one over my left eyebrow is from years of evaluating politicians, and the ones under my eyes are probably from all the tears I shed watching the news. Nevertheless, wrinkles are a sign from God indicating wisdom. Young people *can't have them.*

So now if you agree with me about wrinkles, help me spread a little propaganda to counteract all those dumb advertisements that make elderly people look bad. Go right out and tell your neighbors and your friends, "Wrinkles are beautiful!" Shout it from the housetops. Wait. I better change that for seniors: "Shout it from the window!"

And if this works, perhaps we can suggest "Fat is beautiful!" ...next.

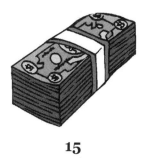

15

Winning the Lottery

The LORD makes poor and makes rich; He brings low and lifts up (1 Samuel 2:7 NKJV).

The lottery has changed from making millionaires to making billionaires in the winnings because so much money is accumulated. Personally, I think I'd be happy with a couple million or so. Wouldn't you? I think most people would. If they'd establish a reasonable limit, maybe the lottery accrual over that could be allocated to help find the cure for cancer. I say spread the wealth for a good cause!

My best daydream used to be what I'd do if I won the lottery. I'd pay off the mortgage, my credit cards and eliminate my bills. It could certainly enhance retirement.

I talked to the Lord about how this could work for good if He'd let me win. I promised to help the poor and not forget my tithe - but it didn't seem to influence Him a bit. I reminded Him that some of His favorite people like Abraham and Solomon were rich. Then He reminded me that being righteous was more important than being rich.

He who trusts in his riches will fall, But the righteous will flourish like foliage (Proverbs 11:28 NKJV).

Back when I wrote a column for the newspaper, I had the opportunity of interviewing a woman (I'll call her "Jane" to protect her privacy) who won over four million dollars after buying a lottery ticket. After I interviewed her and wrote the exciting story which was printed in the paper, she told me "the rest of the story." I've learned getting instantly rich is not all it's cracked up to be.

It was a dark and stormy night. No kidding. The electricity was off for four hours on this memorable weekend. Jane braved the wind and rain to go out and buy a lottery ticket, dreaming of the happiness she thought she could find if she won. The following day, she ecstatically checked and rechecked the winning number. Eventually, it sunk in. She was a big winner.

Jane told me her initial feelings were overwhelming. She shook with anticipation as she wondered how she would spend all that money. Her anxiety was so elevated that she ended up having to get a prescription from her doctor to help her to relax.

After the money was deposited, the management of her new bank account was more stressful than anything she'd ever experienced, and she confessed that in some ways she wasn't a winner. For one thing, she lost the once comfortable, simplicity of her life.

She was able to pay off her debts and buy the house and car of her dreams, but having so MUCH was a nightmare. She admitted the things obtained so easily simply didn't mean as much as the things she had worked for, and her life became cluttered. Ultimately, the experience with winning all that money was definitely not as satisfying as she expected. The fabulous things she bought didn't make her happier.

Losing her privacy, because of all the publicity, took away some of the thrill she once anticipated. Everyone knew she had a lot of money so she received a relentless stream of annoying letters and phone calls from "charity" cases. Even people she thought she knew came greedily to her for contributions. Sadly, her relationships with her boyfriend and other people were negatively influenced by her riches. And although by appearances she seemed to have everything, she admitted becoming terribly lonely.

People didn't understand how she felt and her former friends often found her depressed because she began to think everyone just wanted her money. (They did.) The people who were once dear to her acted differently and seemed to change. That glamourous lifestyle that she once thought would be ideal wasn't as fulfilling as she imagined.

An inheritance gained hastily at the beginning will not be blessed at the end (Proverbs 20:21 NKJV).

The woman I interviewed was being honest. I suppose not every winner has the same experience, but I'm convinced that people who have won the lottery don't really live happily ever after.

I guess winning money won't solve all my problems either. But I hope the Lord will help me find some good sales when I go shopping today.

16

Finding a Little Hideaway

"There's a place for us," the song says, but I didn't used to be so sure; I've always had expectations for the next life, but I had serious doubts about the here and now.

My husband and I changed residences a lot when I was a young homemaker. The moving boxes were barely unpacked before we were uprooted again. I've lived at over 31 different addresses. The longest I ever lived in one place was for 15 years, and it was kinda nice to have a designated spot to put the Christmas tree in December.

Nevertheless, people who know me also know I don't mind moving. I like change. Besides, it gives me the opportunity to redecorate. But recently, Dennis and I decided it was time to downsize, so we started looking at real estate again. Since it's just the two of us in this house, we figured we didn't need extra excess living space to heat, cool and clean.

As we began to look for the ideal setting, we looked for a little place with an ocean view. Regrettably, we learned rather quickly we couldn't afford it. Besides, all the good spots are already taken by movie stars and politicians.

Our next choice was a rustic mountain cabin. It sounded so romantic. But in search for homes in our price range we found ourselves lost on dirt roads so far from civilization we'd sell our souls for a public restroom. We trudged through forests so remote the mailman couldn't find them. The only neighbors would be deer and bears.

In the end, we decided to think more sensibly. For instance, at our age, we shouldn't be far from a medical facility. We even considered a retirement home -but the people living there were much too old.

When the kids and grandkids showed up for Thanksgiving, we took a second look at the space we only *thought* we didn't need. As it turns out, we decided to keep the house we have. Ultimately in our search for a *"little hideaway,"* it seemed impossible to downsize sensibly.

A few months after our agreement to give up on the idea, my husband surprised me by suddenly deciding to spend our hard-earned money for that little place anyway. He tried to explain it was the right thing to do before I blew my top.

He said it didn't compare to the other real estate we looked at and we didn't have to hurry with a down payment because there were only 199 lots left. Furthermore, we wouldn't have to worry about fine print, taxes, depreciation or upkeep in this purchase.

Now I admit... he was right. We have our "*little hideaway*" at last. We enjoy ocean views and mountain landscape from our private entrance. It has been an incredible experience.

I've decided to share our secret because you could probably afford one too. Dennis found it in the top shelf in the sporting goods section of Wal-Mart, just beyond the fishing poles.

We're enjoying our tent! It's a great alternative for retirees who still have the energy to escape now and then ... and if they have a *really comfortable* blow up mattress.

17
My Diet

I'm afraid my taste buds have had too much control of my life. I don't want to be like the people described in Philippians 3:19. Gluttony is an offense I've taken too lightly, and I'm not feeling too lightly. I must control my appetite.

Moderation is better than muscle, self-control better than political power (Proverbs 16:32 MSG).

Obviously, it's self-control that I need, because, actually, I'm an expert on dieting. I've tried all the weight loss programs and battled with the bulge since I was sixteen. Funny, my overweight friends think they're diet experts, too. And I think maybe they are. Interestingly, most of us are thoroughly familiar with the basics of dieting.

Even as a child, before I began using my lunch money for candy bars, I knew which foods were fattening. I learned the importance of each food group early, and throughout my school years, I was taught about carbohydrates, fats, and fast food. But you could say I flunked dieting.

My work-out machines ended up being dust catchers. And when my exercise efforts made me hungry, I ended up at McDonalds. Then a couple months ago, I'm out of the shower and drying off my less than skinny frame in front of a full length mirror. While analyzing my profile, my image clearly sent a message. It was time to deprive myself of decadent desserts.

After I dressed and drove myself to Baskin-Robbins for my "last" indulgence, I came back home and got on the scale - which obviously couldn't be reading correctly. But I determined to make the numbers go down.

This endeavor hasn't been easy. I wake up from noisy stomach growling during the night, and I'm so hungry in the morning I have to be careful to keep from drinking the mouthwash. I suck the coating off my vitamins before swallowing them, and I know how it feels to experience the hunger that makes me even eat the seeds in the apple. Admittedly, certain dog food advertisements make my mouth water.

Diets are torture, but I want to lose weight. Even a few ounces mean a lot. That's why I cut my toenails before I weigh myself. And then I step on the scale carefully distributing my weight. I noticed the scale reads lighter if I stand on it a certain way.

I've had to cut back on everything I used to eat, and I've even had to cut back on watching television commercials. I close my eyes when those advertisements showing plump, glazed donuts or thick, cheese topped pizzas are on the screen. It's too hard to watch. But isn't it interesting that the people in those kind of ads are always skinny?

Even my relationships are affected by my dieting. I became suspicious when my husband offered to take me to dinner at the most expensive restaurant in town - for the first time.   My sister is devastated because I won't eat any of her birthday cake, and my grandkids are upset because I won't use the coupon they brought me for a free giant pizza which expires tomorrow. They *know* I can only eat at restaurants with a salad bar.

Well, I'm getting some good results at last.   I'm astounded to discover I might not have a "large frame" after all. But why is it when I finally begin to lose, it's never my waist that gets smaller? I don't mind buying new undergarments that fit, but I've noticed that even my shoes are becoming too loose.

If I lose five more pounds, I won't be cutting off the size patch on my new jeans this time, and I'll actually weigh what it says on my driver's license.

18

Football Liberation

Football season began as I'm writing this. I hear those old familiar enthusiastic noises that I've heard all my life resounding from the T.V. room. It's my husband I hear with shrieks and moans along with that curious male vernacular as he expresses his joy or lament. The NFL began their thing in September. Hallelujah!

"What?" you say. Surely a woman in her right mind who doesn't know the difference between a quarter back and a full back (their backs look the same to me), cannot appreciate football much. Well, I may not be "football literate" but I see the advantages of the NFL.

I use to hate football when my special dinner preparations got cold waiting for family members to get to the table because they're sidetracked by the game. Even though I've endured many years of social gatherings and holidays being interrupted with blaring television broadcasts and crude shouts of victory or defeat, my view has changed. I don't hate football any more.

Do I like to see football obsessed individuals leaving cookie crumbs in the sofa cushions, pizza sauce on my throw pillows and wet aluminum cans on my coffee table? No, I don't. But this football widow no longer despairs. This is an opportune time, nevertheless.

Nowadays, I'm outta here before the National Anthem is sung. Besides, few performers can sing it without making me grit my teeth. No sir, I do not impatiently sit and wait while a bunch of hunks try to kill each other and destroy a nice lawn between a couple of goal posts.

I don't want to watch a bunch of old men act like young, googled eyed boys glued to the TV while exhibitionists (i.e. sexually unfulfilled) cheerleaders jump around in their risqué get-ups making spectacles of themselves to get some attention.

Some wives choose to spend half the season waiting for halftime, but I want more than half the time. To me, football season represents give and take. I give my husband the living room and I take the credit card.

I'm more understanding at the mall and I'm free to shop 'till I drop! After all, this may be the only time HE suggests it. I can't help it if a man may feel a little guilty for ignoring his wife during the game. Of course, if he's too preoccupied to suggest it, I watch for the moment when he grips the armchair or when the score is tied. That's when I hit my precious couch potato for some cash for shopping. He doesn't argue a bit.

I've also learned to suggest ordering dinner so I don't have to cook during game times. Some wives already know this. Did you know? More pizza is sold during football season than any other time.

I used to think football was in the same category as "the other woman" with that "rival" demanding too much time and attention. I don't remember a problem before we were married, but I wouldn't be surprised if something was *going on* behind my back even then.

Football has seduced a lot of men, but it won't be my home wrecker, and there's nothing wrong with getting a little something for my sacrifice. Besides, Macy's is having a sale!

19

Is the Honeymoon Over?

. . .For your love is better than wine. (Song of Solomon 1:2 NKJV)

Dennis and I celebrated another anniversary recently. I guess we were supposed to have candlelight and champagne, a romantic night on the town and all. Instead, we had a rather mundane evening together, doing what we wanted . . . which wasn't much.

The fact is, we just stayed home and watched an old movie on TV. Then, as I sat in my comfy old bathrobe, stuffing my face with popcorn, I looked across the room at my inattentive husband, snoozing on the couch. I began to wonder if the honeymoon was over. Had we lost the passion we once had? Maybe. I decided I better take a closer look at our life together.

I walked into the bedroom and looked in the mirror. Appraising my less than alluring image, it was clear the woman I saw in the reflection didn't look anything like the girl my husband married. The one who looked back at me was two dress sizes larger and her face looked like a "before" advertisement for Botox. Nevertheless, I knew it took more than a diet and a face lift to keep passion in a marriage.

The more I thought about it, the more I wanted to epitomize what a good marriage needed, and grabbing a pencil, I started a list: Love, commitment, unity, patience, trust, communication, self-control, gentleness... As I wrote, I realized my list couldn't cover everything concerning what couples needed for a good marriage, so instead, I decided to make a list of a few good things we've had in our marriage.

We laugh together. We kiss each other. We can talk about anything. He keeps gas in our car. He sings to me in the shower. He likes my cooking. He puts the toilet seat down (usually). We share everything from the bank account to the bed blankets (usually). We may have disagreements, but we ...well... that's all I'm going to say about that.

That list appeared a little puny too. But at least I knew for sure if I had to go back and do it again, I'd still marry Dennis. And if I were stranded on a desert island with one person, I'd want it to be him. But I still didn't have the answer I wanted for whether or not the honeymoon was over.

Finally, when Dennis stirred from his nap, I asked him if he thought the honeymoon was over. I had to ask him twice because he was still half asleep. With a surprised look on his face he finally said, "Of course the honeymoon isn't over if your wife makes you dessert, even when she's on a diet," and he laughed. It was probably a hint.

Leaning on a pillow, he paused a moment as he studied my serious face, and continued, recognizing I might need some reassurance. (And incidentally, everyone should give reassurance sometimes because everybody needs it - even old married couples.)

Briefly, Dennis said, "If your wife washes your clothes, sews on your buttons, prepares your meals, gives up the TV for Monday Night football, gives you a back rub, still wants your hugs and kisses, and most importantly... if she leaves you alone so you can sleep on the couch when you want to, then, it's not over!" Then he smiled sleepily at me, rolled over on his stomach and went back to napping.

I can't explain it. But I knew for sure. His few words reassured me and I knew the honeymoon wasn't over, just by looking at his contented face.

Next year, maybe we'll go out to celebrate our anniversary. But whether we do or not... the honeymoon isn't over because we have what it takes.

Love suffers long and is kind; love does not envy; love does not parade itself, is not puffed up; does not behave rudely, does not seek its own, is not provoked, thinks no evil; does not rejoice in iniquity, but rejoices in the truth; bears all things, believes all things, hopes all things, endures all things (1 Corinthians 13:4-7 NKJV).

And that's the epitome of it all.

20
Me, Myself and Him

Psychologists generally agree it's healthy to talk to yourself - so that's my excuse.   Anyway, I personally think it's good for me to get my ideas and feelings out and offer myself some positive feedback. Sometimes that's hard to come by through anyone else.

I've been talking to myself all my life, but lately more than ever.   Some people think age has something to do with it.   I like to think that it's just all the wisdom that spills out of us as we mature. Besides, we're not supposed to hide our lights under a bushel.   Still, I admit, with all this talking, it makes me think I might be getting a little senile.   I saw this kind of senility in my grandpa when I was younger, and it could be hereditary.

Years ago when I was a kid, I remember looking out the kitchen window while I was washing dishes. I noticed grandpa on the front porch, enthusiastically scolding someone; however, he was quite alone.   I silently watched until curiosity overcame me. Sliding open the window I asked him, "Grandpa, who are you talking to?"

"Your grandma," he replied, pleased that someone asked.

"But ... grandma is in the house," I said as I turned to look towards the other side of the house behind me. Grandma was seated in the living room.

"Yes, she is," he said impudently, "but this is the only time I can get a word in edgewise." He laughed hysterically.

Despite family history, I maintain that talking to myself has value, even if some people have a problem with it and think I'm loony. I guess my husband has the most problem with it. He finds it hard to differentiate whether I'm addressing him or me.

It began when we were first married. He walked into the room while I was having a terrific conversation. To avoid embarrassment, I told him I was praying. Of course, eventually, I was forced to tell him the truth since my conversations weren't always very . . . spiritual. I explained that writers particularly need an outlet of expression by talking to themselves. My husband told me I expressed myself plenty, but he understood why I wanted to talk to myself. That way I'd be sure to get the answers I wanted.

Anyway, over the years, when he's confused about whether or not I'm speaking to him, he has learned to patiently ask, "Was that question for me or you?"

I've read that people only hear about 50 percent of what's being said to them anyway. So it's great to be one's own sounding board. Still, we can't take ourselves too seriously. Sometimes I have to let my words go in one ear and out the other. Nevertheless, there is something powerful about hearing what you're thinking.

I think everybody needs to have this regular experience. It has great value. For instance, if you can get your feelings out and inspect them while you're alone, your words won't do the damage they might do if someone hears them. It's best to hear yourself first. And it's amazing what you'll discover if you listen.

A good man out of the good treasure of his heart brings forth good; and an evil man out of the evil treasure of his heart brings forth evil. For out of the abundance of the heart his mouth speaks (Luke 6:45 NKJV).

We ought to have a serious talk to ourselves about that.

21
The Perfect Job

At last, as a senior citizen, I've finally obtained the job I often fantasized about as a young adult. Back in my youth when my employment working conditions were far from perfect, I daydreamed about the ideal job.

I pictured a workplace where I had my lovely, private office with all the files and supplies I needed, a copy machine and the controls for the air conditioning next to my big, beautiful desk. Also idealistically, the coffee maker, a refrigerator with cold drinks, a pantry for snacks and a comfortable couch for naps would be nearby. Beautiful music would play through the speakers in the room, and maybe even a television for use during breaks.

I wanted every holiday and all weekends off, and of course, the boss would be nice. He wouldn't get upset when I stayed on the phone with my friends too long. The dress code would be casual and I could even take my shoes off and work barefooted if my feet hurt.

You might be thinking, having a job situation like this would be impossible, but now I've got it. Actually, I've had it quite a while, with all the benefits I dreamed about.

Among other things, my office is arranged just the way I want it and my favorite music plays through the speakers on the bookcase. I'm often dressed in an old pair of jeans and a t-shirt and my shoes are off right now. I talk on the phone with friends any time and I take long breaks.

I quit working my other jobs a few years ago to do something I'm a lot happier doing, even though I don't actually get a paycheck. Have you guessed? I'm retired, and any work I may have is right here in my home.

Interestingly, not all women, especially the younger ones, feel the same joy that I do for home sweet home. They'd rather have a job outside of the house and get a paycheck so they can buy gas, pay the babysitter, find a house cleaner, go out for lunch and purchase a lot of clothes for work.

The title of "Homemaker" withstood the disdain of many in the twentieth century, and it is still an anathema to some women. They've scornfully found the mundane tasks of housekeeping and child raising beneath their dignity. It's unfortunate that they don't recognize the great significance that goes with this job description.

The Bible encourages women to be discreet, chaste homemakers (see Titus 2:3-5), but in this day and age, full time homemakers are practically extinct. Although I do believe some males have found refuge in posing in that traditionally female station.

(Notwithstanding, I don't believe man has the inherent makeup for this task.)

Of course I understand that it's necessary for many women to work outside of the home - like I did for some years. But now I have the perfect job!

This very week I had a great time doing things like passionately shaking cleanser in my sinks and making them shine; going outside to wash the back windows with a hose and drying them off with wadded pages of the newspaper; tucking fresh-smelling bedsheets onto our bed, tenderly placing fluffy clean towels on the towel rack, unloading sparkling glasses from the dishwasher, setting a pretty table and preparing appealing dinners bringing tantalizing aromas to our home.

So there you have it. I'm a Homemaker and proud of it. It's a different life from the rat race I was in as a young woman.

This is the life. I have the perfect job! The only thing I'm wondering about is . . . what am I going to do tomorrow?

22

Threads

I was standing in the kitchen cutting carrots for my famous beef stew when I heard hysterical laughter resounding from the living room. Peeking around the corner, I spotted my 19-year-old granddaughter, Nikka, dangling her legs over the side of the recliner and sitting in one of those strange positions that only kids can manage. My high school yearbook was open in her lap.

Eventually she looked up and saw that I was watching her. "Grandma," she said between hysterics, "I can't believe you ever looked like this!"

"Is nothing sacred?" I asked while she continued cackling and turning the pages of the album.

I glared at this girl with black and purple fluorescent checkerboard fingernails, a green streak of color in her hair, stained jeans with holes precisely ripped in them, half a blouse exposing her belly button, an armful of very weird bracelets and six earrings flopping on her shoulders with each wild giggle.

"Your clothes were so creepy, Grandma."

"Look who's calling the kettle black!" I exclaimed and returned to my stew, stewing.

Nikka followed me into the kitchen with the yearbook and pointed to a photo. "Who's that dogface beside you?" She continued muttering her impressions while I looked over her shoulder noting that "dogface" was her grandpa in younger years.

"Peel the potatoes honey," I ordered. She put the yearbook down and moved to the task at hand with a bewildered look on her face.

"Grandma, did you wear dresses to school every day?"

"Yes, I did."

"Did you like wearing dresses?"

"I didn't think much about it at the time...but it was nice that everyone could be able to tell the girls from the boys."

By the time the stew was ready and the table was set, we had spent a good portion of the afternoon talking about styles. I even pulled out an ancient Sears and Roebuck catalog to show Nikka what people wore in the "good old days." I noticed that she seemed fascinated with women's dresses and even showed interest in my views concerning the effect that more feminine dressing has upon the opposite sex.

After I went to bed that night, I began thinking about the styles that have come and gone over the years. (My clothes closet is a wonderful example.)

Although blue jeans have been a popular mainstay since Levi Strauss patented them in 1873, jeans have been available in various designs. We've had boot cut, flares, baggies, hip huggers, bells, pre-washed, pre-shrunk, acid washed, bleached, slimmer's, stretch, striped and streaked, all in every color and texture imaginable. And certainly, designer jeans must have changed the economy.

Miniskirts have been my least favorite style since I've never liked my knees much. The longer the skirt is the better. Remember the muumuu? It was like a skirt that began at the neck. Nobody knew when I was up a few pounds. Those were the days.

It's a shame when older women try to keep up with clothing trends. I personally like to cover as much as I can with a pretty, flowing, colorful, loose-fitting something. Actually, one of the few stylish things I can find that fits that description is my bathrobe, but it's inappropriate for social functions. It has become more difficult to find clothes I like.

Women's clothing displayed at the stores tends to be racy, tight fitting, in flimsy see-through materials. I'm convinced that they only make woman's underwear for hookers and girls who weigh less than 105 pounds.

I remember the day when a lady wouldn't go out of the house without a girdle, not to mention a bra, but that was when it was chic to have a little meat on one's bones. The bra is back in style again despite the bra-burning era, but now they're wearing it on the outside.

Men's clothing doesn't change as radically as women's. Consider the necktie. How on earth did this item become so popular? Nevertheless, it doesn't matter a bit how popular, my husband won't wear one. And I don't see too many at church anymore.

It's confusing to figure out fashion. Perhaps there's something to be said for nudist colonies. But the Bible tells us that God made coats of skin for Adam and Eve so apparently nudity wasn't what He had in mind.

Even though clothing had a modest beginning, people quickly became flamboyant. They didn't even get out of Genesis before Joseph had a coat of many colors.

My granddaughter's generation seems to think "Anything goes." Still, it surprised me when I saw Nikka in a pretty dress a couple days after our conversation. She admitted that her boyfriend really liked it.

23
Traffic jam in the jelly section

Seniors should never, never, never do grocery shopping on a Saturday if you can help it. Believe me, I know what I'm talking about.

Saturday is when all the people who work on weekdays do their shopping, and the stores are jam packed. You can bet your burger buns that Coupon Day is risky business too, but Saturday is out of the question. Actually this retired person won't be caught dead in the aisles after 11 a.m. any day. It's just not safe. But foolish me, I fought the fight last Saturday and live to tell about it.

I ran out of peanut butter. I needed it for the peanut butter cookies that I promised to the sixth grader's class at church on Sunday. I told myself I'd just dash in and out. But I found myself caught in a maze of people at the grocery store, most of whom were oblivious to the frustrating delay they were causing those of us who have better things to do than spend their lives gripping the handle of a grocery cart.

One step at a time, I worked my way through the crowd. I saw a few inches of clearance and attempted to blaze a trail with a like-minded, haggard shopper following dangerously close behind me, But I soon found myself behind a row of indecisive cereal pickers.

Then, up ahead a child driver with an ulterior motive, knocked down an Oreo cookie display. I watched the cookie monster being scolded by his mother who actually seemed indifferent to her son's continued reckless motivation. I couldn't pass through until the floor was cleaned without eagerness by an overworked clerk.

Finally, pressing forward, I sighted the shelves with strawberry preserves, knowing the peanut butter had to be near, but a young couple was dilly-dallying near the apricot pineapple jam, so I had further delay. I patiently waited among the rapidly growing, antagonistic throng while the couple determined what they ought to have on their toast. Each jar was evaluated ever so elaborately for all to hear, and I wondered how they would deal with more important matters in life.

I only wanted one jar of peanut butter. "Choosy mother" or not, any brand would do. But there was a group of ladies in my way and they were obviously completely absorbed in conversation. I waited a little while, but finally, I abandoned my empty shopping cart and ducked between the group of talkers, squeezing around them to get nearer the right section.

A toddler sat in the shopping cart near my destination and began spilling an open box of Lucky Charms cereal on the floor. Nevertheless, I plowed ahead without hesitation, even though the sticky cereal stuck to the bottom of my shoes as I grabbed a generic jar of peanut butter.

Moving back through the oblivious group of ladies again, I barely managed to recover the empty grocery cart which was almost lost to a younger shopper who, due to the shortage of carts that day was getting ready to steal it. But with the barricades still growing, I didn't want to lose it. I thought pushing it might give me some leeway as I advanced to the check-out line, so I quickly grabbed it. She probably gave in to me because I was looking so old and haggard by now. (Have you ever noticed how self-centered attitudes in over-crowded stores are contagious?)

Almost there at the checkout, I whirled around and a large lady with a toothy smile accidentally bumped into my cart with hers. A chubby little girl was sitting in the basket, sampling the groceries. "I guess there should be stop signs in the aisles," the mother chuckled, taking a chocolate candy bar from her daughter and placing it back in the rack half-eaten.

"I wish there was a fast lane," I said as the woman snickered at her kleptomaniac child groping for another item from the shelves.

Then I saw the talker lady group slowly manipulating their shopping carts towards the cash register, so I moved posthaste to the check- out line before they could block my passage again.

Someday I'd suggest aisle signs to the store manager like "NOPARKING" or "YIELD." But as I waited in the 10-items-or-less line, I realized how silly it would be to erect traffic signs in the store. Obviously, few people could read.

When I finally found my car in the parking lot, I noticed an innocent looking elderly couple looking for a grocery cart. Regretting my selfish behavior to the woman who needed it in the store, I pushed the cart towards them in penitence. But before I got into my car, I warned them. "Sorry to be so blunt, but if either of you have a problem with high blood pressure, you better wait and do your shopping on a weekday morning."

24

Voicemail

I suppose most business can be taken care of (sooner or later) over the telephone. But it's so hard to get to a live human being who can answer your questions or give help. I hate listening to those lengthy, recorded messages telling the caller which numbers to push to get to the right department. It seems like I never get there.

Insurance companies, the DMV, doctors' offices, and the Social Security Administration especially try to use up my remaining life on the phone. It's just not right.

If God intended for us to spend our lives on the phone, he would have made our ears differently. I studied myself in the mirror the other day and noticed my left ear is shaped differently than my right ear. This is presumably from the many hours holding the phone on my ear in attempts to get to the person that will give me the information I need. The Surgeon General should put a warning on telephones that says, "Warning: This telephone may be dangerous to your ear." Anyway, I'm inclined to think that people who let their fingers to do the walking are disillusioned.

Monday morning, I called the bank to ask a question about my account. The elaborate automated message began with, "If you want to continue to hear the message in English, press one, now." "If you are calling to open an account...." "If you are calling to order checks ..." on and on it went. You know how it works. You've probably been there.

To save time, I began loading my dishwasher, holding the receiver with my shoulder against my deformed ear. (Now that I think of it, my left shoulder is a little different than my right one.)

"If you are calling about a loan press..." I kept pressing numbers with hope that eventually I'd get to a human. Meanwhile, I started studying my index finger. I'd never noticed. It seemed to be bent differently than my other fingers. Hmm.

After more questions, at last I heard "If you want to speak to a customer service representative, press ..." Elated, I pressed the right number and heard, "If you'd like to speak to someone about ...." Here we go again.

Finally, I thought I'd connected to a person. Instead, it was another recording. "We're sorry, we are experiencing a large number of calls, there are no customer service representatives available at this time, but if you choose to wait ..."

I waited. My dishwasher beeped and I began unloading it.

Eventually, an operator came on the line, I thought. But it was another recorded message. "Please press the last four digits of your account number."

How could I have forgotten? I immediately began frantically searching for something with my account number on it. The long telephone cord followed, displacing my desk calendar, dumping the pencils and pens from my pencil holder, emptying the pencil sharpener, amputating the top of a house plant, and sending my desk lamp flying. With the phone cord wrapped around my legs, I found the account number. I knew if I ever called the bank again, I'd use my cordless phone.

Composing myself, I took a deep breath, wiped the sweat from my brow and unwrapped myself from the python cord before I attempted to punch in the correct numbers with my weird looking finger. It was then I heard that all too familiar shrieking that occurs when the telephone is taken off the hook for too long.

There wasn't a terribly long line at the bank, for a change. I approached the only teller as she looked at me curiously and sympathetically asked, "What happened to your ear?"

25
Stress

Writers should write what they know. If you've read the previous chapters, you know...I know about stress. There is good stress and bad stress and I've had both. And I'm pretty sure you've had both.

Without stress there can't be growth and life. Nothing will grow or live unless it has movement. So we need stress. You probably didn't want to hear that, but I'm mentioning it because this fact is uniquely significant to elderly people in retirement.

One's amount of movement and continued growth (i.e. inevitable stress) is a factor in how long an individual will live. How often I've seen people who finally retire, stop living...literally. Even plants and animals (along with people) must move and grow to stay alive.

Fortunately, the bad kind of stress can usually be avoided, yet curiously, plenty of people regularly indulge in it. There are thousands of familiar methods practiced by psychopaths with occasional encouragement by psychiatry, but the following things are a few of the basic elements of bad stress which can make any normal person batty.

Bad stress happens when we allow things like negative words, ingratitude, self-pity, laziness, gluttony, envy, greed, hatred and unforgiveness into our lives. Indulging in this kind of stress will give a wretched life and an early grave. It spoils anyone by emptying them of purpose.

Good stress is not as easy to get. Usually work is involved and ambitious people have a lot of good stress. Again, it's obtained through growth and movement. Among other things it includes thinking on good things, patiently listening more than talking, forgiving one's enemies, giving thanks, not comparing oneself with anyone and loving and serving people.

Now as for my personal experience with stress, I'm grateful that most of the bad stress I've experienced isn't too serious. Like that day my bra clasp broke while exercising in my coed senior's calisthenics class. It wouldn't have been so terrible if the left breast padding hadn't dropped to the floor while I was doing those dreadful jumping jacks. I gave it a swift kick as nonchalantly as possible. Then aghast, I watched the unidentified flying object being recovered from the swimming pool with much conjecturing by the rescuers. I hastily jogged to the locker room, admitting nothing.

It was bad stress on the day I turned the wrong way on a one-way street because I thought it was a short cut. The cop was going the right way. It didn't matter to him I was running late. In my hurry that same morning, I accidentally passed my house mistaking the neighbor's place for my own. It was also bad stress for the neighbor when I admonished her for parking in front of "my garage." Well, our houses do look a lot alike.

Of course, good stress is easier to take. It's when I only have three sit-ups left out of the ten that I told myself I'd do. It's when I watched the only horse I ever bet on come into the lead while still only halfway around the track. It was good stress the day I dropped my wedding ring in the toilet but managed to pull it out before I flushed. It's balancing the checkbook with twenty bucks remaining instead of being overdrawn.

Good stress is nervously kneeling at the altar on Sunday morning and feeling like people are wondering what you did wrong. It's confessing your sins to God and knowing that He will forgive you and alleviate your bad stress.

We can choose good stress or bad stress every day. Like I said, I've had plenty experience with both. But when I've made the wrong choice, I know what to do.

Casting all your care upon Him, for He cares for you (1 Peter 5:7 NKJV).

26
Beauty or the Beast

It's said that beauty is in the eye of the beholder, and I'm saying that the old woman I'm beholding in the mirror isn't the real me. I'm the same person as I was when I was 21 - I just need more makeup.

Frankly, I depend on cosmetics when I want to look my best. I don't believe in all that "natural beauty" stuff. There aren't really many natural beauties. I know. I've been with women in beauty salons, locker rooms and weekend camping trips.

Beauty is an illusion and I have to work at it. Revlon helps me out a lot, (not to mention Playtex). The way I see it, by looking at the billions of dollars in sales of beauty products (and the bottles, and jars, and tubes, and sprays, and powders, and soaps, and creams stacked up in my own bathroom), beauty isn't just "skin deep." It's a lot deeper than that.

I'm sentimental about my very first tube of lipstick. It smells kind of funny now, but it was a godsend over sixty years ago. Boys began to notice me.

It's still incredible what red lips will do to the average male. They don't think about whether beauty is "skin deep." The truth is, they're impressed by skin...even though they have no idea what women do to get it to look that way. And most women will probably go to great lengths to make ourselves look as good as we can until we're on our deathbeds. I kinda think that's why so many of us choose cremation. Nobody else could possibly ever get the makeup right.

Keeping ourselves looking good in our senior years (and actually most of our lives) has been torture. We pluck our eyebrows, tease our hair, shave our legs, pierce our ears, peel our faces and steam our bodies. We endure starvation, aerobic exercise, hot hair dryers, burning curling irons, smelly hair coloring and permanents. We've worn everything on our face from mud to mayonnaise and clog our pores with eye shadow, foundation and miscellaneous contaminants.

After inhaling excessive amounts of hair spray and perfumes, we stuff ourselves into tight pants, cinch our waists with belts and hang various rocks and metals on our bodies. With heavy bags on our shoulders (which is actually the reason shoulder pads came into style), we walk out of the house on stilts, all while trying to ignore the stiff wires under our bosoms.

Sometimes I envy my husband when it comes to the lack of fussing he needs. His wardrobe is simple with a few shirts and pants. He doesn't have much hair on his head to worry about. He takes a quick shower and applies a little after-shave, and that does it.

Still, I'm glad to be a woman - and glad I've known some marvelous beauty techniques. It only took me several years in high school to learn most of what I know, but I could write a book about it now.

I'd begin with a chapter teaching girls about using ordinary household items in their beauty regimen. Vanilla flavoring is a nice scent to use if you run out of perfume. Frozen persimmons work well for puffy eyes. And just like mother said, your eyes will be brighter and your skin will glow if you eat your fruit and vegetables.

There are little timesaving things I learned over the years like, it's a waste of time to curl your eyelashes before you say your prayers. Or, don't cream your hands before you floss your teeth. As a young homemaker I learned not to do my nails before preparing meatloaf. My father-in-law never forgave me after he almost swallowed an acrylic fingernail.

I'm much older now than when I first began using makeup. I'm afraid the end result of my artistry isn't as great anymore. But I still make an effort. I'm thankful for a 10x's magnifying mirror that helps me see a little better so I can put the makeup in the right place, more or less.

I'm a sight for sore eyes before I get ready to go out in public. Recently, Dennis caught me after I'd rubbed a green facial mask over my face. I had a plastic, purple flowered shower cap over my hair. It was strange hearing a grown man scream, but when he realized it was just me, I smiled exposing the whitener goop on my teeth and said, "Look for the inner beauty, honey." He hasn't looked at me quite the same since.

27

Do You Know Where Your Children Are?

I was a Family Day Care provider back in the seventies. This was back before the government imposed incredible "safety" stipulations and dictated what children "needed" for nourishment and a "healthy" environment.

Anyway, even though my playroom wouldn't have met ADA requirements nowadays, I treated the children who were in my care like they were my own (and they were healthy and happy). I loved them dearly, and although they were only mine for a few hours each week back then, I still have a habit of calling them "mine" after all these years.

The other day, my cousin, Cheryl, and I went to visit our friend who was in the hospital. As we were getting on an elevator that was packed with people, I noticed the parent of a child who had been in my day care. I remembered his name was Jim, so I told him hello. He politely nodded at me as we shuffled into the crowded elevator.

As the elevator ascended, I really put my foot in my mouth when I introduced him to Cheryl. It seemed that everyone in that congested space was listening to me as I announced to my cousin, "This is the father of one of my twenty-five children."

There were gasps from the people standing around us, but I hadn't realized the implications of what I'd said. Cheryl later informed me that she'd seen their horrified glances, along with the father among the horrified. He had attempted to respond to me since I spoke his name, but no words came out of his mouth in his astonishment.

I thought his bewildered expression was due to not being able to recognize who I was - I've changed a little since the seventies. But at the time, I just blundered on, oblivious to what I had implied.

"You probably don't remember me, Jim. I only spoke to you once or twice." More gasps were heard.

I watched the now pale-faced, dumbfounded father nervously swallow and shake his head as our audience watched. Then the elevator door opened and he quickly moved out without looking back. I still didn't get it.

Perplexed at his behavior, I told Cheryl, and the listening audience who really seemed quite interested, "Once in a while I see some of the other fathers, but most of them recognize me." She looked back at me with wide eyes as if she was beginning to choke on something.

After a few seconds of silence, and the elevator door closed and began ascending to the floor of our destination, my cousin fell into rather loud hysterics.

Distracted by her demented laughter, I didn't use the opportunity to explain things to the remaining elevator passengers, but it was obvious that several remained horrorstruck by my confession.

Later as I thought back on the scenario, I was comforted knowing that we were not far from an emergency room in case Jim couldn't recover himself from the elevator revelation.

And just in case someone reading this knows the man to whom I'm referring, please assure him for me. He doesn't owe me any back child support. Also, for the sake of my own reputation, my children and their father know each other very well.

28
Saga of a Breast

The lovely, curvaceous female body seems to be worshipped by the American culture. Shapely hips, small waistlines, sexy legs, voluptuous breasts, and seemingly perfect figures appear in fashion shows, movies and magazines (but not in my neighborhood).

The contours above the waist are given particular notice and ridiculous value is placed on the fatty tissue in the mammary glands. Since so much importance is placed on external endowments, most women panic at the thought of losing a breast. So did I when I thought I had breast cancer, and the forty-eight hours until I knew what must be done were filled with anxiety.

Clenching a pink tissue as I entered the clinic, I remembered the day long ago when I stuffed my thin, beginner bra beneath my white blouse with the same. Later, after enduring the snickers of a couple heartless boys, I'd wished I had used white for the effect.

I signed the doctor's appointment sheet and sat down near the magazines. There was a women's magazine with busty models in bikinis on the cover on the top of the stack so I turned it over and picked up a National Geographic.

The nurse opened door number one and called a name. A woman in a high-necked outfit got up. Probably not her first visit.

The National Geographic magazine had pictures of African women with exposed, healthy breasts. I didn't need more reminders so I quickly exchanged it for a safe-looking family publication. The first article was about the advantages of mother's milk.

Reminders of the lump in my breast were everywhere. Trying to get my mind off of it, I picked up a Gideon Bible laying by the stack of breast magazines and opened it up, avoiding the Song of Solomon.

Before I could concentrate and change my thoughts, my name was called. That was certainly quicker than usual. For previous doctor appointments, I had sat in the reception area so long I thought they forgot me. Maybe I was an emergency case.

I followed the nurse through antiseptic smells to a pale green room where she clunked and balanced metal pieces on a scale to register my weight. She asked, "What seems to be the problem today, Mrs. Young?"

Looking at the reading on the scale I said kiddingly "I'm at least 15 pounds overweight and I'm afraid it could be this lump in my breast." Even though she gave me a half smile, the nurse didn't seem to think it was funny. Neither did I, but she got the picture.

She handed me a thin, blue paper gown and ordered me to undress, disappearing before I had a chance to ask if the gown opening was in the front or the back. I never could remember.

I sat down on the cold leather and chrome exam table, crinkling the oversized frock around me. It was quite full of wrinkles when the doctor finally arrived -not to mention the extra ones that came to live on my face that week.

The doctor asked me many questions such as, "When did you first notice the lump? Is it painful? Has it changed?" After his examination, I was told to get dressed and take some paperwork that was marked "Expedite" to X-ray.

After another of the longest hours in my life, I sat in another pale green room with another unflattering paper gown and looked at my white goose-bumped legs. I really needed a sun tan but I'd given up sun tanning because of the danger of skin cancer. Now I wondered about the danger of x-rays.

After being pushed and positioned while the cold mammogram apparatus clicked for pictures, I asked the technician for a blowup copy for my husband. Nobody had a sense of humor in this place. I meant the left one I urged.

I was given an appointment with the surgeon in the same complex for the next day. I slept little that night.

The waiting room was crowded that morning, yet I found a seat near the usual inadequate reading material. But I didn't take a chance on it. I'd already spotted statues of naked Greek goddesses on the cover of one magazine. Instead, I tried not to think about that awful thing in my breast by watching other patients and imagining why they were here. But it worried me that the waiting room was emptying of people and they weren't coming back. Had they seen their end on the operating table? I concentrated on the people left in the room.

Perhaps the lady with the limp needed hip surgery. A huge man with large rolls of fat sat between two seats. Probably here to get it cut off I thought just as his eyes met mine. I tried to control the feeling that pulled at the corners of my mouth when I realized that man might be speculating about me. And so was that woman...and others were staring.

I crossed my arms and began to think the magazines might have been a better option than watching people. I fidgeted for a pen and notebook in my purse and wrote down ideas for a tragic novel.

I was dabbing my eyes with a tissue when at last my name was called. My audience watched as the poor woman with the cancerous breast followed the nurse.

I was given a blue paper gown but this time I knew the opening went in the front. While laying on my back, I felt the small alien nightmare that had trespassed into my breast without permission. I had decided I wanted to go home and die in my own bed when the doctor entered. Seeing my tears, he said, "Don't worry. We often see small tumors like yours."

As I lay looking at the glaring light paneled above me, I felt the needle of a syringe being inserted with a quick, sharp jab. I felt a heaviness within my breast as the tissue was deadened. I closed my eyes afraid to look at what came next, but the surgeon's positive words made me open them again.

"Good. This is what I thought. It was only a cyst, Connie." There was a slight indentation on the surface of my numb breast where the deplorable lump had been.

I joked with the nurse while she applied the Band-Aid. "I hope he didn't take too much."

As I started to leave the clinic through the back door like everyone else, I turned around and returned to the front area to reassure the somber audience - and I said, "Hallelujah, I'm healed!"

29
Hoard and Seek

My parents lived through the hardships of the Great Depression (1929-1939), so it was no wonder that they raised me with the "Waste not, want not" concept. Their teaching stuck with me all these years, and because of that fact, I drive myself a little crazy trying to find a use for *everything*. I'm afraid that saving items from the garbage isn't exclusively an eccentric idiosyncrasy of the bag lady.

Among my collections, large and small, are furniture, toys, pop bottles, mayonnaise jars, old magazines, rubber bands, paper clips, photographs, ribbons, dishes, books, bags, boxes and buttons to mention a few things.

I'm particularly fond of collecting clothes with hope they will come back in style – and better yet, fit me again. Shoes are another weakness. My foot size has been the same since high school, even with these bunions. I actually have a couple pairs that I've owned since then, and they're coming back in style - along with a lot of things.

That which has been is what will be, that which is done is what will be done, and there is nothing new under the sun. Is there anything of which it may be said, "See, this is new"? It has already been in ancient times before us (Ecclesiastes 1:9-10 NKJV).

Sooner or later, everything seems to come around again. So I store things away, *somewhere*.

My husband isn't exempt from a hoarding tendency either. He keeps paint, pipes, doors, hubcaps, matchbooks, baseball caps, golf balls, football memorabilia, coffee cans, nails, washers, screws and tons of tools and car parts. His clothes closet is full of raggedy t-shirts that he won't give up. And strangely, he has an enormous collection of keys in the top drawer of his dresser for which he has no idea which locks they fit. At least I only keep what is useful.

Well, the Bible tells us to be good stewards. In some cases, there may be a fine line between hoarding and good stewardship. Actually, "Hoarding tendency" may be the wrong phrase to use concerning our collections. We're just over the top frugal. Our children will confirm that fact; of course they live in a generation that thinks everything is disposable. I don't want to be that way, but it became clear we needed to remove some of the clutter.

Salvaged items had accumulated everywhere things can be stored in this house. Useful or not, stuff clutters up our lives, not just our closets. Something must be done if it's difficult to find things because there's too much collection. Furthermore, it is extra work keeping things organized and clean when one has too much, and a house stuffed to the brim can be a fire hazard. So, I began the giant task of eliminating stuff.

First, I called the kids, hoping they'd take some of the more valuable things off our hands. After all, as I explained to them, each item has a unique history. I thought they would surely appreciate our generosity. But they didn't. I was appalled to discover our children had no reverence for our treasures.

"Sorry Mother, I hate Victorian furniture."

"Those dishes are lovely, but they can't be used in the microwave."

"Why would we want 25 photo albums of pictures when we have all our photographs on the computer?"

"Those clothes are too old-fashioned for me."

"If it isn't plastic, your grandkids will break it."

"Keep my crib? You've got to be kidding."

"If those knick-knacks were in our house I'd have to dust them."

After giving up my attempts to teach my adult children the worth of priceless things and understand my sentimental values, we decided to have a yard sale.

It was hard to watch my precious articles sell for so little - and after all the years I stored them. At the end of the day, my apron pocket held only a mere eighty-three dollars and thirteen cents. Many things to which I had attached to fond memories were gone, and my heart was a little broken.

Meanwhile, my husband had been reading something that was written on a piece of paper that fell out of one of the books we sold. He handed it to me without a word, and then he began pushing the leftover sale items into the garage.

"Do not lay up for yourselves treasures on earth, where moth and rust destroy and where thieves break in and steal; but lay up for yourselves treasures in heaven, where neither moth nor rust destroys and where thieves do not break in and steal.

For where your treasure is, there your heart will be also (Matthew 6:19-21 NKJV).

After we finished moving the remaining, inevitably perishing items into the garage, we called the Salvation Army for pickup.

My closets and shelves were roomier for a while. But I've noticed things are definitely accumulating again.

30
Cabbages and Kings

When we were close to retirement, Dennis and I downsized to a smaller house and yard. Fortunately, the front yard was landscaped when we bought the house. We both used to love gardening, but our shoveling arms aren't what they used to be, so we were happy to see that the front yard looked presentable right away. On the other hand, the back yard had an incredible crop of weeds, including the interesting ones that sprouted under the bird seeder.

As far as Dennis was concerned, the back yard wasn't a problem. It was his retreat. His home is his castle and the back yard his kingdom. He has a large comfy hammock strung between two posts where he reclines and reads Louis L'Amour books and dreams about Colorado. There's a barbecue grill and a table big enough for his iced tea glass. These were the only items among the weed jungle for a whole summer after we moved there.

He liked to stretch out and gaze at the sky without contemplating disturbing subjects like sprinkler systems, lawn mowers and weed killers. He figured he had already spent enough years being overly concerned with that kind of stuff. It's important to rest and "Take time to smell the flowers," but there were no flowers that summer.

Funny, the things you learn about the person you thought you knew after years of marriage. I had no idea the same man who used to bring me roses when we were young happens to hate rose bushes.

Dreaming of a not-so-secret garden with glorious flowering plants and trees, I showed him the marvelous pictures in gardening magazines, hoping he would be inspired. My vision was uprooted when Dennis told me what he envisioned was a place where our great grandchildren could dig in the dirt without plants to worry about. I expressed my need for violets, and he stressed conserving water. I pleaded for gardenias and he reminded me of his allergies.

He had an argument for everything, but at last he agreed to compromise and begin working on the back yard in the spring ... if I would allow him to make the choices in plants. Little did I know what he planned.

When spring sprung, he was unusually enthusiastic about the yard. Busy with other things, I didn't pay much attention when he returned from the nursery. He had dirt on the knees of his overalls when he came to get me to see what he'd done. He'd decided to landscape our back yard entirely with food-producing plants and trees.

I was impressed, and I imagined the savings on our grocery bill if everything growing was edible. Aesthetically, fruit and nut trees are just as beautiful for landscaping as any tree I've seen. Pomegranate trees look fabulous with their red buds. I've always thought peach trees were lovelier than pines, and

I've seen an avocado tree that grew as tall as an evergreen.

At last, our backyard is something to behold. Our shade trees produce more than shade. Among other delicious victuals, berries grace the trellis and the walkway is lined with bright green peppers. There are melons instead of marigolds, parsley instead of petunias, cabbages instead of camellias and turnips rather than tulips. Is there anything as pretty as a ripe, red tomato? And well, I decided that strawberries are better than having roses, after all.

31

Four Eyes

They've been a thorn in my flesh since I was a kid. At the same time, I know they're a blessing and I shouldn't complain. Without them, I'm almost blind. So I do thank the Lord for eyeglasses, even though I've had some negative experiences.

It began when I wore my first pair to elementary school. My classmates pointed at me and laughed. I didn't understand why my mother thought I looked "so pretty" in them while my classmates seemed provoked to fits of giggling and insults.

I soon learned that eyeglasses were inhibiting when I played sports. And when I was trying out for cheerleader, it was embarrassing when they bounced on my nose when I jumped. One day I took them off for a swimming tournament; I didn't properly judge the distance to the pool edge and conked my head on the siding. It was just a scratch but I was disqualified. The judges didn't want blood in the pool.

After all these years, I still don't like the way eyeglasses feel when I wear them. If I could find a pair that didn't have to rest on my nose and leave dents, I might be okay.

I'm one of those people who can't stand things like earrings that pull on my ears, hats that push my hair flat or heavy jewelry hanging on my neck. I even cut the tags off my clothes so they don't scratch. Remember the story about the princess and the pea? I have similarities when it comes to small irritations.

I've tried contacts, but they smother my eyeballs. And radial keratotomy surgery is a marvelous alternative but I'd have to win the lottery first.

Along with being forced to wear something across the major part of my face, those tiny screws come loose when I'm doing things like mixing the meatloaf, playing a piano solo or eating greasy barbecued ribs. And those who wear glasses understand the annoyance of how they get fogged when we remove food from the oven or dishes from the dishwasher. Then there's the problem of keeping the darn things clean. How can I clean them if I can't see without them?

I like color coordinated outfits when I dress up. I'd like to change my glasses like I do clothes, but I only have a couple pair of glasses to work with. Actually, I'm ready for a new pair.

Last week at the mall, I thought I saw a friend from church standing inside the large window of a store. I gave her a big smile and waved like mad as I approached. I felt so foolish when I finally became aware that I was grinning like an idiot at a mannequin.

My husband thought I was kidding about my eyesight because I wanted another color coordinated pair. But after I screamed and scared him when I found a strange looking "insect" in my pantry, he couldn't deny my need for new glasses any longer. He rescued me from a raisin.

In the hilarity of his discovery, he forgot that he left a can of Black Flag on the pantry shelf. That can has a remarkable resemblance to the cooking spray can. Good thing my nose still works right.

Shortly after that mistake, Dennis drove me to the eye doctor, indicating I was his blind date. It was a foggy day, and I realized after all, there might be some worth to those signs over the freeway confirming the fog, for those of us who don't trust our eyes any more. Tax dollars at work.

My exam indicated my eyesight hadn't diminished as much as I feared (but I'm still getting new pink framed glasses).

Leaving the exam room, I clumsily bumped into the door as I was exiting. The doctor stuck his head around the corner and quipped, "I'll put a rush order on your new glasses, Connie."

32

Wrong Side of Sixty

Unless you're under the age of thirty, you'll probably identify with those of us who occasionally get the blues about our age. I won't elaborate on what makes us depressed because if you're a senior, you already know. Even Job Longed for the days gone by (See Job 29:2). It isn't always easy to grow old gracefully. Of course there are a few optimistic individuals who say they don't mind getting old. But I don't believe them.

My husband, Dennis watched me frowning at myself in the bathroom mirror just the other day. "What's the matter with you?" he asked with a sarcastic tone, knowing exactly what the matter with me was as I scrunched up my face, inspecting the crow's feet around my eyes.

I glared at him and quoted the old saying, "If God had to give a woman wrinkles, He might at least have put them on the soles of her feet." I pulled a kinky grey hair out of my once natural blonde head with a tweezers, noting it was time to color again.

"Why are you doing that?" he audaciously snapped while looking at my reflection in front of his own salt and peppered head in the mirror. "We've earned our grey hairs. The Bible says, 'The silver-haired head is a crown of glory.'" (See Proverbs 16:31.) He lovingly spit-placed a straggling white whisker in his beard.

I earned them alright, but I thought only my hairdresser should know for sure what I've earned. Then seeing me pout, he said gently, "You look young for your age." Whereupon, I immediately called the salon for an appointment. Mark Twain said, "When people begin to flatter you on how young you look, it's a sure sign you're getting old."

My preoccupation with the signs of aging began earlier this week when I was shopping. I ran into this kid I used to babysit when he was a mere toddler. He introduced me to his grandson. There must be some mistake...or maybe I shouldn't be wearing my hair in a ponytail anymore?

I wandered through the stores morbidly imagining my hair in a bun like my grandma wore. As I walked passed the toy store in the mall, a mechanical parrot whistled at me, making me feel lighter on my feet. I went into the store and bought the darling little bird on the spot. Of course the bird is motivated by movement and it would have whistled at my ex if he walked by; nevertheless, it made me feel better ... for a while.

I know a woman who got a face lift to make her feel better because she was going through a "mid-life crisis." Hah. I've had one crisis or another all my life - so if that's the only one she experienced, she's lucky.

Imagine if the aging process was backwards and we were born with wrinkled skin and saggy whatnots. Then as we mature in wisdom and experience, we'd look better and better, until at last, we retire with someone to change our diapers, feed us and take care of us. (Well, I guess there are some similarities with how it is.)

Anyway, certainly senior citizens would get more recognition, parents would find it easier to control misbehaving children, and perhaps I would eventually beat my son at ping pong.

An old friend of mine told me if I just keep "growing and learning" as I age, I'll become more authentically myself as God intended. Well, I've grown a lot around my middle, I'm authentic enough, and frankly, I've learned more than I want to know. Still, there's something to what she said.

Another one of my peers said the medical journal is beginning to look like a book of memories and she regularly checks the obituaries to see if she's dead. I've heard that before, and the obits are too depressing. Besides, people don't really die in alphabetical order like the listings make it seem.

Other friends wish that things were still like "the good old days." Not me. They didn't have acrylic fingernails, microwaves and nonfat ice cream back then.

I actually don't feel much different than I did as a child. That is, on the inside. Although Christmas comes a lot sooner now. And I guess I haven't aged chronologically anyway. People are supposed to get smarter as they get older, but I knew a lot more when I was a teenager. I don't know what happened. About the time I lost what I believed was exceptional insight, my parents became incredibly wise. And I should mention, nowadays, I see my grandchildren as extraordinarily brilliant.

33

All scream for ice-cream

I'm on a diet again. "What else is new?" my husband asked. Well, this is new. I'm going to stop indulging in the largest source of my fat and calorie intake. I'm going to give up ice cream.

My favorite food in the whole world has got to go. I've actually waited too long to give it up. It's a pity. "A moment on the lips, forever on the hips," as the saying goes. There have been many, many moments.

Giving up ice-cream might not be a big deal to some people, but for me, it ranks in importance right after my firstborn and just before my other relatives. So you can see this will be a major sacrifice.

When I'm dieting, I can generally resist other desserts. Although I love all the fat people's favorites, I don't have an uncontrollable weakness for things like biscuits and gravy, pizza, or chocolate. Okay...maybe chocolate.

I quit cigarettes many years ago, but that surely wasn't as hard as this will be. I definitely think the Surgeon General should place caution warnings on cartons of ice-cream too.

I LOVE ice-cream. I eat it every day. I'm too embarrassed to tell you exactly how much ice-cream I eat, but I should tell you if you've invested money or bought stock in ice-cream products, you better cash out as soon as possible. Ice-cream sales are going to decline drastically. And I don't need to invest any more around my middle.

Because I've succumbed to incredible mouth-watering flavors like Jamoca Almond Fudge, Rocky Road and Moose Tracks, it will take some time to lose that investment. For years I was beckoned by decadent packages of Brownie Madness, Berry Cheesecake and Cookie Dough.

Ice-cream is responsible for the fact that I don't fit half the clothes in my closet. When I first came to this realization, and in attempt to cut back calories, I tried limiting myself to vanilla. But I soon learned moderation isn't the answer for me. Somehow, plain vanilla ended up being covered with chocolate syrup or nuts or something else to make it more exciting.

Then I tried all the low-fat and nonfat concoctions that looked like they might be edible. One spoonful eliminated the potential for future purchases. I'm an ice-cream connoisseur. And, I'm afraid, an ice-cream addict.

I don't know of any organizations that offer rehabilitation for those of us who struggle with this addiction. I'd like to find a lovely place in the country where I could escape from places like most grocery stores, Baskin Robbins and the malicious ice-cream truck man who is aware of my addiction. My ears hear the tinkling of his music from the speaker of his truck, miles before he gets to my neighborhood. When he gets to my block, he has the audacity to park in front of my house.

In order to have successful recovery from my addiction, I must stay away from ice cream parlors, food stores with frozen dessert sections and birthday parties. There will be no more apple pie a la mode, hot fudge sundaes, or my favorite Pistachio Nut ice cream cones scooped for me at the drug store. My life will be changed.

That's "will be" you know. I'm afraid seeing all this in print got my craving going. Besides, I'm just preparing myself, psyching myself out before I begin. And there's only a little Pralines and Cream left in the freezer. Somebody's got to eat it.

34
Christmas in July

I'm going to gripe about something that I've been noticing in otherwise nice neighborhoods in my community for quite a while. It's a pet peeve for which I've needed to vent since January - and now it's July.

The thing that bugs me is that I'm still seeing houses and yards decorated for Christmas. It's just not right.

I love Christmas. I love Christmas decorations. But not when the weather is over 90 degrees outside and the neighbor kids are wearing shorts, getting tans and taking swimming lessons. Rudolph should be at the North Pole along with the other reindeer. Sleighs and elves shouldn't be popping up in unkempt yards, and Frosty the snowman isn't compatible with summer vacations.

I don't want to have to look at those strings of fake icicles and yellowed snowflake things, glowing in the sun and hanging off the neighbor's fascia. Especially not on a warm day while I sit on my porch drinking iced tea instead of eggnog by the fireplace. Besides, I had enough of seeing incredible numbers of those manufactured things everywhere back in December. They look like a disease.

I can see Christmas lights with dangling cords strung on the eaves of a few houses down the street from me. There's a star on one rooftop, plastic objects peeking through trees and faded decorations here and there. What is the world coming to?

When I was a kid, Santa Claus didn't show up until the annual downtown Christmas parade. If my recollections are correct, most people didn't hit the Christmas tree lots until the first weekend of December. In fact, back then all signs of Christmas disappeared by the end of January. It's not like that anymore.

Nowadays, Santa and the yuletide glitter adorns windows, department stores and parking lots long before my tomato plants finish producing. And the decorations are up for so long - they have to be dusted for spider webs regularly. One might say holiday decorations have become ho-ho-hum.

Christmas decorations used to be fun and exciting to see, celebrating the birthday of Christ. But seeing them in an inappropriate season make them unappealing. The only good thing about them is that they remind me it's probably really a good time to start shopping for Christmas presents.

35

People

As I remembered the people who crossed my path over the years, I noticed certain personality types kept appearing. In every group or setting, whether at the job, in the neighborhood, at church, or wherever I went, certain types showed up, sooner or later.

Classifications of people like I'm talking about aren't the descriptions one finds in psychology or psychiatric studies. I know there's supposed to be four basic personality types for instance; however, I see a different assortment of characteristics.

Notwithstanding, despite observations herein, it's impossible to "classify" a person completely. Only God can do that.   But with that said, I think you'll still see the understated categories that I will describe bear the resemblance to many. And although these individuals have countless names and faces, their behaviors are uncannily similar.

I add a disclaimer here to assure you that the following names are fictitious to protect the identities of the people repeatedly appearing in our lives. Furthermore, although they may have certain offensive idiosyncrasies, this is a matter of nonjudgmental consideration.

I first noticed the **Kay Ottick** personality at my workplace in my younger years. She's the type who was always terribly busy and buried with responsibility. The only bare spot on her cluttered desk had a splotch of nail polish and some cookie crumbs. If I came across some irritating paperwork I was tired of dealing with, I gave it to Kay. I'd never see it again. Her crammed desk contained items like expired discount coupons, hardened sticks of gum, and scraps of paper with unidentified phone numbers. It didn't contain an ink pen that worked or a clean envelope. Her home was much like her desk when it came to remarkable conglomerations.

Slow moving, slow talking **Jerry Attrick** has been around since the war. There has been speculation about which war, but nobody lives that long. Besides, I think I went to high school with him. Jerry hates change and refuses to use a computer because he thinks it's the Antichrist. Jerry demands your attention and respect. He lives in the past and will tell you about the "good old days," but if he's already had an opportunity to tell you, you've already heard it all. He is one of those people who can tell you exactly what he was doing when Kennedy was shot because he's still doing that. He's not a bad guy unless you're in a hurry.

Perfectionistic **Percy Veering** is a workaholic and a dedicated company man. He dresses meticulously, his home and yard are picture-perfect and his vehicle shines like it's just been polished. It has. It's difficult for Percy to tolerate any kind of sloppiness. Precision and Punctuality are important to him. His only vice is his addiction to antacids. So if the form indicates he's supposed to get the yellow copy, don't give him the pink. The paramedics are busy enough.

Percy's counterpart, **Sandy Dandy** makes most women look bad in comparison. She's thin and gorgeous with perfect nails, perfect hair and perfect teeth. I think I went to high school with her too; however, she undoubtedly had a face lift. Sandy is gifted. She can do anything better than anyone else. She always knows what to say and keeps a beautiful smile on her lovely face. One would think there are never any problems in her life. Men adore Sandy and women envy her.

Ann Tagoniss hates Sandy, and everybody else, actually. She's the most critical person you ever met and discourages those who are trying to do their best. She trusts no one and particularly dislikes church people. You better not talk to her about her need for God, unless you're willing to face her scorn. In her opinion, Christians are hypocrites. Ann watches every move people make deriving morbid gratification when anyone screws up. Meanwhile, she won't lift a finger to help. If looks could kill, Ann would slay thousands.

Madonna Backstab is Ann's ally. Her sweet expression keeps people from suspecting the nasty things she is whispering to Ann, but she's a wolf in sheep's clothing. She may be two-faced but no one is certain what the left side of her face looks like because her cell phone is usually in front of it. Madonna loves gossip. If she appears to be quietly meditating, she's probably eavesdropping on the people behind her.

Al Most is a "wannabe." He may be a gang member, the boss' brother-in-law or the cop who pulled you over for driving two miles an hour over the speed limit. He tries to usurp authority in attempt to be important, but to his dismay, people tend to ignore him. Nevertheless, he doesn't give up and continues to be insistent, even in petty matters. Al is quite opinionated and supposedly experienced in so very many things. Underneath the facade is a sad man who feels that life has passed him by.

Adam Bomb behaves like a pushy, temperamental child most of the time. He may be the president, a deacon in the church or an inspector for the planning department. His outbursts intimidate the people around him and strangely, he gets his way most of the time. He manages to get cooperation through yelling. He's really not a happy man and there's an "I'd rather be fishing" sign on his wall. Most everyone wishes he was.

After being around Adam for very long, **Flo Onandon** is almost a pleasure. But she has a horrible case of logorrhea and is an unrestrained chatterbox. There are few pauses between her words, so when you see she is turning a little pale, you may have to remind her to take a breath. Still, she has good things to say if you have time for a talkathon. There's really not more to be said about this type. Besides, she'll tell it all to you anyway.

I've only mentioned a few personas, but since I'm not ready to start another book just yet, I'll end with these. And incidentally, there's no use changing your job or your church or your neighborhood to avoid the ones with whom you cannot abide. The Lord has a purpose for them.

As iron sharpens iron, so one person sharpens another (Proverbs 27:17 NIV).

That verse explains why certain types have crossed my path. Through them, among other things, I am taught patience, self-control and unselfishness. I'm still being taught. But you knew that. Anyway, that's why even though the faces are different, they keep reappearing.

Relationships are the most important thing in life, beginning with our relationship to God. As we grow in that relationship, our relationships with all kinds of imperfect people will get better too.

36

Lazy Days of Summer

I have sweet memories of my childhood, especially summer time.

Our family trips to the mountains are the most memorable. When school was out, we gathered our camping gear. Dad tied most of our supplies, the sleeping bags and the tent on top of the station wagon and hung a water bag on the grill. (We didn't have little plastic bottles of water back then.)

When we arrived at a campground, we pitched our tent and settled in for a few days. A clothesline was hung between a couple trees with a blanket to provide a little privacy, and a place to dry our wet swimsuits after swimming in the lake. We cooked our meals on the campfire, some of which were dinners which Mother had pre-prepared at home, but all which seemed to taste better while dining outdoors in the mountain air.

We collected pine cones, hiked, fished, climbed rocks, watched for deer, and occasionally heard of a bear alert from the Forest Ranger, making camping even more thrilling as we hunted for bear prints.

At night around the campfire, we roasted marshmallows and shared silly stories (which ultimately inspired my writing career). We sang songs like *Row - Row –Row Your Boat, B-I-N-G-O,* and *"Mairzy doats and dozy doats and liddle lamzy divey..."* and laughed until tears streamed from our eyes.

When we finally slipped into our sleeping bags, we fell asleep gazing at incredibly bright stars in the sky, listening to the breeze moving through the pines and hearing night sounds of nature.

I remember anticipating those special weeks of summer vacation which would bring that special camping trip and other things. Other things like swimming pools, baseball games, bike rides, roller skates, tree houses, wiener roasts and ice cream cones.

Those simple things were the greatest pleasure in my life, and frankly, I never had my fill. I have hope that the next life will bring similar delight. But not everyone sees it that way nowadays.

RV's seem to be more popular than tents. Families are more likely to book a hotel with an artificial playground and a swimming pool rather than go to a campground without Wi-Fi. Besides, one can't cook a TV dinner over a campfire anyway.

Today, families with school children have a different summer than we had. I'm inclined to think that the negative implications with the kids out of school are more than a higher electric bill. When it's over, parents deserve t-shirts or bumper stickers that say "I survived summer."

My neighbor's children wine, "There's nothing to do." These are the families who have a swimming pool, over 100 channels on the television in their bedrooms, remote control everything, endless video games, laptops, cell phones, untold sports equipment, a gymnasium one block away, a neighborhood park on the corner and 19 other neighborhood kids with similar stuff.

I remember complaining that I was bored to my mom before summer ended. I thought she'd help me out. She did. But after I finished those chores, you can bet I found plenty to do on my own.

They finally taught kids to "Just say no." Now if they would also teach them to say yes. On the other hand, I'm told that parents apparently have not learned to "Just say no" because children could threaten their unreasonable parents by calling CPS if they're trying to discipline them. Alas.

Well, I'd love to have one more summer vacation with my "unreasonable parents." Thank God they knew how to raise me – even though there were many times when I didn't get my way.

This year my summer vacation will consist of spring cleaning my house. I'm running a little late. I don't have the energy I had as a child when I was climbing those wonderful rocks in the campgrounds.

Hikes to the mountains are a thing of the past. Even a stroll down the road has its terrrors... (Ecclesiastes 12:5 MSG).

37

Lost and Found

I believe in the supernatural. Some things can't be explained any other way. Not just the Divine supernatural. For instance, I lost my glasses yesterday. Again. Every now and then they disappear. I looked everywhere. But it's hard to find something when you can't see very well without that something.

I've experienced the mysterious disappearance of other items in this house too. Books, scissors, forks, pencils and pens have turned up missing the same freaky way. The TV guide and the clicker are the most commonly missing items. Food items, especially ice cream, seem to evaporate right out of the freezer. It's bizarre.

Pillows and blankets vanish in the middle of the night. Towels abscond while I'm still in the shower. Interestingly, other people, at least the married ones, say they've also experienced the same darn thing. It's uncanny.

A typical example of this kind puzzling vanishing happens on wash day. You've probably had this happen too. Socks are put in the laundry basket with all the other clothes to be washed. Somewhere, between the laundry basket and the clothes dryer, they go. I don't know where. I have a drawer full of socks that don't match.

The reverse, the curious *appearance* of certain items is just as unexplainable. One or two of my husband's old, worn-out shirts keep reappearing despite the many times I've thrown them out. Sometimes I find coins, buttons and paper clips in the bottom of the washer after it is emptied of clothes (but no socks).

Have you ever wondered why there are crumbs in the silverware drawer? Even if you don't believe in the supernatural, you can't deny that those particles strangely appear there. It's a common phenomenon in households everywhere.

Whether it's a certain photograph you thought you destroyed, a past due bill you've never seen before, or more hairs that suddenly turn gray on your head, it's unnerving to have these kind of things unexpectedly appear.

Another frequent peculiarity regularly happens around meal time. The house is quiet and empty. You pull dinner out of the oven or take the meat off the barbecue. Then you sit down at the table anticipating a quiet meal, and at the exact time, the phone rings or certain people inexplicably, coincidentally appear at your front door.

Well, at least I finally found my glasses yesterday. So that's one mystery that was solved. Actually, Dennis found them after I complained that I'd lost them. It's a little embarrassing to admit, but I hadn't thought of looking for them where I pushed them on the top of my head.

38

To Be or Not to Be

"To wed or not to wed?" That was the question they asked me during a singles class at church that I happened to interrupt. I had no business being there except that I was looking for pencils for the senior's class. I remembered seeing a package of yellow/gold number twos in that room. I tiptoed into the room as these vivacious young people were discussing the pros and cons of marriage.

Knowing that I'd celebrated many years of marriage, they thought they could get some input, so they cornered me before I could get away. Then they jokingly fired questions at me and insisted that I give them my viewpoint - so I succumbed to their request.

I didn't feel it would be right to be careless with the subject, though it wasn't easy to admit the fact that I had been married twice. So up front, I admitted that I had experienced both an inexcusably failed marriage (I know God forgave me but I can't justify failure with excuses) and a successful marriage. In between, I enjoyed living as a single adult for a number of years.

The group was all ears when I told them being single has some benefits. The Bible tells us even the angels don't marry (Mark 12:25), so being single must be good. I told them I loved my independence, my tranquility, my TV shows. I didn't have to put up with the stuff that wives endure like finding a sticky tube of toothpaste squeezed in the middle, toilet tissue missing or hung backward, whiskers stuck on the soap and towels that smelled like car grease.

When I was single, I didn't fight for the newspaper, the checkbook or the recliner. I ate ice-cream out of the carton, flipped the television channels to my heart's content and slid the thermostat control up or down as I wished. Nobody yelled at me when I had cold feet in bed, onion breath or spent too long getting ready to go someplace. I left late or early for an event, or changed my mind and stayed home without having to explain. I didn't want to prepare twice as many dinners, wash twice as many dishes and have twice as much laundry to do. They laughed when I said usually, even if a husband is willing to help, unless you want live on pizza, have the dishwasher loaded like a garbage can and find your underwear the same shade as your red towels, it's better for a wife to do those things herself.

After I shared the benefits of being single, I was a little concerned while watching a girl who was frowning and twisting off her engagement ring. I tried to think of appropriate Bible verses recommending marriage, but there seems to be more verses advising a believer to remain single. And other scriptures seemed to be a bit one-sided.

He who finds a wife finds a good thing, and obtains favor from the LORD (Proverbs 18:22 NKJV).

But what does a wife find? Hmm. I decided to stick with the positive.

I told the class that it has been proven that life expectancy is greater in married people - but just be sure you know what is expected. And I mentioned the fact that there isn't tremendous social pressure to marry anymore. Couples often choose to live together as an alternative for marriage. But that is unacceptable. Hebrews 14:4 explains that marriage is honorable, but God will judge fornicators and adulterers. Because of sexual immorality, Paul suggested in his letter to the Corinthians, "... *let each man have his own wife, and let each woman have her own husband.*"

Before I left the room with the pencils, wondering if I should have run away when I had the chance, I told them that I could highly recommend marriage if they found the right person. Nevertheless, one doesn't fall up when falling in love, and no parachute on earth can keep you from falling. And in my opinion, wedlock is deadlock.

Marriage isn't a 50-50 proposition. It requires 100% by both parties. Then I reminded them, most importantly, a good marriage takes three. It takes a miracle from God in order for any two human beings to live happily together all their lives.

In retrospect I realized, it was a tough subject on which to comment. But I prayed that these kids wouldn't be so quick to jump into marriage like many in my generation seemed to do. And perhaps while you're reading this, you too will pray for the young people you know who may be considering marriage.

1234567890

39

Number, please

Years ago, when social security numbers were first assigned, there were people who emphatically resisted being labeled with a number. I can understand that.

The people who objected to this method of identification were those whose reasoning was not merely because they didn't want to be impersonalized with a number, but also because they thought this numerical tag came from the devil. I can understand that too. Little did they know that social security numbers were only the beginning.

Nowadays, numbers are used for everything. And numbers are attached to numbers. For instance, I have several credit cards, all of which have a lengthy number. On the back of the card, there's another number. Besides that, for added security, I have a personal pin number.

In many instances, our language has changed from words to numbers when we communicate. We can punch in numbers when we do things like check our bank account balance, get money at the ATM, make credit purchases, disarm the alarm, use voicemail, open the gate or door, and in a variety of other circumstances. Because of the massive use of numbers, there's less interaction with human beings than ever before.

Anyway, my problem with numbers is not fear them I'm going to be identified with the devil, but I'm having a devil of a time remembering the darned numbers. It's troublesome enough just trying to remember the numbers for the correct coffee filter size, my sister-in-law's birthday, and my age, just to mention a few numbers cluttering this elderly mind.

All these numbers make my life confusing – especially when I do business over the phone. For instance, a few weeks ago, I received an invoice from my cable provider which I thought I'd already paid. So I got on the phone and called the company to check on it.

I was forced to listen to one of those nightmare recordings that when on and on, reminding me at intervals that they would soon have an operator available. It certainly wasn't soon, but a human finally spoke. Well, I think she was human.

"What is your secret four-digit number?"

"What secret number?" I asked.

"We need your secret four-digit number," she repeated.

"I don't have a secret four-digit number," I responded. "I only want to know if there is a balance owed on my cable bill."

"I'm sorry, but this is confidential information," the voice intoned. "I need your secret four-digit number."

I laughed. "I think my secret four-digit number must indeed be confidential information - because I don't have it. I just want to pay my bill. Can't you tell me how much it is?" The operator didn't laugh and repetitiously repeated her request without compassion.

I tried guessing at what might be my "secret four-digit number" using the usual dates, weights, ages to no avail. Exasperated, I threatened to discontinue their cable service. But it didn't help.

I was flabbergasted when she said, "In order to disconnect your service, I must have your secret four-digit number."

We won't be watching Jeopardy tonight. My husband said he thought something was wrong with the television. But it's not my fault. I really tried to check on my cable bill.

40

Painter's Plaint

I'm not a good painter. I've painted this and that, a chair, a picture frame, my fingernails, but I end up getting more paint on me than the items I'm trying to paint. And after the last experience with painting, I don't ever want to paint again.

My husband, Dennis and I decided to paint the underside of the patio cover. We chose a dark paint color to reduce the glare. Despite Dennis' sighing, it didn't look like a big deal to me, with only 196 square feet of shiplap to cover. I chuckled and told him it didn't seem like much compared to Michelangelo's project of 6,000 square feet of ceiling in the Sistine Chapel.

Dressed in old clothes and armed with a paint brush, I slowly climbed the ladder, still unaware of the magnitude of the task. Dennis, not as inexperienced in painting as I, curiously stared at my jolly demeanor as he held the ladder.

Admittedly, after a short time of aiming my once white chin in a direction that became increasingly painful to my once white neck, my disposition took a turn. (Incidentally, I've decided never to dye my hair darker since I've already seen the unbecoming color change.)

After a while, breathing those paint fumes through my once white nose affected my mind, because when the phone rang, I got off the ladder to answer it without considering that my fingers looked like I'd been playing with finger-paints. But any excuse to rest my neck was welcomed.

By the time I'd figured out how to painstakingly get into the house without touching anything, and place my ear in the proximity of the receiver, the caller hung up.

Leaving the once white phone off the hook, I returned to the project finding Dennis on the ladder making better progress than I had made. But calamitously, I bumped into the ladder upon which he was standing, causing the can of paint which was balanced on the same, to dump onto the concrete below as Dennis stared in mortification. You could say, the *gravity* of the task was now apparent.

My dog, Sadie, seemed to have good intentions of trying to retrieve the can for me. This should explain the little nose marks which decorate the French doors, among other abstract art designs and conversation pieces that are scattered in our back yard.

Obviously, the project took longer than I anticipated. My great granddaughter grew an inch in the interim. Now I understand why it took Michelangelo several years to finish his paint job.

When our painting project was completed at last, the market had been changed on paint thinner, and we had sacrificed towels, washcloths, luffas, a bottle of skin softener and a lot of shampoo (including some for a dog who still smells like turpentine). Next time, we'll call a painter.

Just imagine my embarrassment at church on the following Sunday when during prayer, I happened to place my finger tips on my elbows, whereupon I felt hardened chunks of paint I'd missed.

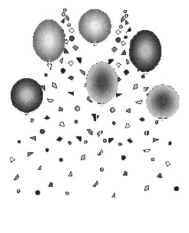

41

Holiday Hullaballoo

Every holiday has a commercial emphasis. The marketing gurus conjure up something for every occasion. Of course, the ultimate purpose of their displays is to get us to spend money. It works. They know how to capitalize on all the seasonal events.

You've probably noticed that the actual meaning of the date we commemorate isn't always what is highlighted by the guys whose primary concern is sales. Retail misinterpretation for Easter is an example. Jelly beans and bunnies certainly aren't my idea of the Resurrection of Christ. But at least we're reminded that an important day is coming, even though empty tombs and crosses aren't used in the advertising industry. (Not to mention the sad fact they are forbidden in many public places.)

The nature of the beast doesn't appear so large at Thanksgiving, although marketing doesn't stop in November. But how much clout can a turkey have anyway? I guess that's a silly question to ask during an election month. But of course, Christmas is around the corner so advertisers are concentrating on the big bucks. Usually candy canes, wreaths and yule décor are imposed long before Halloween.

Still, I have to admit I'm a sucker for all the stuff anyway. I buy all the goodies, including the valentines, the shamrocks, the fireworks, the pumpkins, the centerpieces, the greeting cards - and my charge account budget is maxed each New Year's Eve.

Nonetheless, I'm quite aware that commercialism has profoundly affected our customs. I'm afraid some people are so brainwashed with the sales propaganda that they forget the real meaning of the holiday. If you are among the few who know exactly what we're celebrating, try asking a child (or sadly, an unchurched individual under the age of 40) what the day means and you may be shocked.

Kids especially often have a hard time putting the details together. One little boy excitedly explained that it's Santa Claus' birthday in December. I asked him if he thought Santa was born in a stable. He advised me, "I think that's where he got Rudolph."

Sometimes I think as seniors we particularly have a lot of work to do in sharing the facts. We may be the only ones left who know them. I don't know if it's because our youth have forgotten what is true – or sadly, maybe they haven't heard the truth from us.

Only take heed to yourself, and diligently keep yourself, lest you forget the things your eyes have seen, and lest they depart from your heart all the days of your life. And teach them to your children and your grandchildren (Deuteronomy 4:9 NKJV).

The world with all its hullaballoo doesn't define the truth.   I don't begrudge the marvelous fun included in the celebration of the holidays, but as a result of all the pressure to shop 'til we drop, our culture has become materialistically fatigued, and we've forgotten things of importance.

42

Dinnertime

Sometimes we fail to recognize the small details of life that make us happy. My husband brought one such particular detail to my attention recently.

He was gone most of the day and had just returned from helping a friend with a project. After he peeked under the lid of the pot on the stove to see what I had prepared for dinner, he glanced at the table where I'd already placed our plates and silverware for the meal.

It made him smile and he said, "It has always felt good to come home to a table set for dinner."

Who would think the sight of simple plates, knives, forks and spoons on the table could warm our hearts? But indeed, there is something precious about a table set for dinner, and his comment triggered good memories.

Our children no longer live with us because they're grown up and have children of their own, but we remember the special times our family came together at dinnertime. Those brief minutes in the evenings of our family life were precious – and continue to be precious when there is opportunity for them to come and visit nowadays.

I wouldn't trade those times for the chance to eat at the best restaurants in the world. No matter if the plates are paper or fine china, the dinner table at home has an implicit message that no restaurant can offer. "I belong here. This is my place."

As our own parents taught us, we begin mealtime with thanks. Each of our children had the opportunity to pray over a meal. It was a learning experience for them to practice articulating gratitude and speaking to God. Praying with others listening wasn't foreign or uncomfortable to them in future settings.

We tried to make the dinner table a safe place of unconditional love and communication with our children. Dinnertime provided a space for sharing and listening. Somehow, it always seemed to be an outlet to release feelings, perspectives, good and bad news, along with a lot of teasing and joking.

I began setting the table for dinner as a child, about the same time I learned which hand was left and which was right. The correct placement of silverware was significant to gaining this knowledge. It also became my esteemed responsibility at an early age to place the napkins, glasses, salt and pepper shakers, and the butter plate on the table. To this day, the dinner table looks incomplete without all the above.

The meal has been the center of planning for most family events including birthdays, celebrations, announcements, holidays and various get-togethers.

Most of us would be a few pounds lighter is this weren't customary; nevertheless, the dinner table holds many fond memories.

I'm looking forward to that special day in November when all of our family will meet together. I picture the famous Norman Rockwell Thanksgiving table scene with turkey and all the trimmings, family members young and old, seated around with glowing faces. Meanwhile, Dennis inspired me to regularly set the table for dinner, even if it isn't a special occasion.

It's 5:00 and he should be coming inside to wash-up any minute. I've already set the table for two, and I've even added a couple of pretty candles for effect. Even if the pizza won't be delivered until 5:30.

43

Little Jewels

Julie was my best friend from the time we were both three years old. She had marvelous curly, red hair; and freckles all over her chubby arms and legs. My parents and her parents were best friends also, and we all went to the same country church, so we had many opportunities to be together.

We used to sing a song in Sunday school that pertained to the treasures of scripture with the line, "Little jewels, precious jewels." Mother said I'd look happily at my little friend and beam. It was years before I realized we weren't singing about little Julie, precious Julie.

As children, Julie and I did magnificent things together, but we didn't have television, video games or computers until years later. But we flew kites, rode swings and climbed trees. We walked through mud puddles and ran through sprinklers. We lay on the ground flat on our backs, chewed on a piece of straw and found elephants and angels in the clouds.

We spent blissful hours doing simple things like watching a sow bug make a trail in the dirt, observing a robin building her nest, or making fabulous mud pies and decorating them with pomegranate flowers. We draped blankets over the picnic table to make a playhouse, and collected cardboard boxes to make a train. We depended on our imaginations to entertain us and developed a sense of wonder with life, and somehow, everything was an adventure as we anticipated surprises... and found them. (Perhaps this is a secret of youth.)

Julie and I spent many afternoons catching polliwogs. We caught hundreds of black, slippery tadpoles that looked like watermelon seeds swimming in the pickle jar we filled with muddy water. One weekend our families returned from a camping trip to find an awesome number of baby frogs in the laundry tub where we had forgetfully left them.

We ate splendid things like smelly black licorice, fat red jawbreakers and snow cones that dripped blue ice. Sometimes we chewed on sweet carrots pulled from the garden or sucked on a plump tomato. We licked the egg beaters after mother mixed the cake batter, followed by a cold glass of milk which had arrived that morning on the doorstep in bottles from the dairy.

We put taps on our shoes so we could hear our feet click when we walked and danced, and we drew chalk squares on the sidewalk so we could play hopscotch. We didn't have money very often, but when we did, the finest things were purchased at the corner market. This included pink bubble gum wrapped in wax paper comics or a bottle of cream soda. Any leftover pennies were spent on miniature toys or candy that spilled out of those captivating globe-shaped vending machines. But there was plenty to do if we didn't have any change to spend.

We always had rubber balls, jump ropes, jacks, marbles and roller skates in our glorious treasury. Our toy boxes contained, plastic tea sets, Yo-yo's, color crayons and paper dolls to mention a few valuables. Raggedy Ann and Andy sat on our beds along with all the large and small stuffed animals that we could collect in our young lives.

We traded hundreds of comic books, dozens of pretty rocks and innumerable secrets. We sold lemonade, cupcakes and Girl Scout cookies. When we went for walks or rode bicycles anywhere and everywhere, we always looked on the ground for coins, bottle caps, or perfect leaves and flowers to press within a book for keeping until they crumbled.

On cold winter days, we stayed indoors and played games like Old Maid, Pick-Up Stix and Mr. Potato Head. Sometimes my brother let us use his Erector set, and we built incredible cabins and fences for our dolls with his Lincoln Logs and Tinker Toys.

Tears fill my eyes as I think of these truly grand memories, such free and joyful days of childhood.

I write these recollections in loving memory of Julie, my precious jewel of a friend, who surely waits for me to come and play - in Heaven.

He will wipe every tear from their eyes, and there will be no more death or sorrow or crying or pain. All these things are gone forever (Revelation 21:4 NLT).

44

Paper or Plastic?

There are many imitations and counterfeits in this world. It seems everything can be reproduced, deceiving our eyes into believing it's the real thing. Movie makers are particularly adept at creating images that appear authentic. We're never certain about what we're viewing, making it harder to trust anything we see on the screen.

One imitation that I've had problems with comes at Christmas. I guess it's kind of silly, but I never liked artificial Christmas trees. Man-made, manufactured ones simply don't have the same appeal as God-made ones.

Our children were brought up appreciating the beauty of a live tree. We have wonderful memories of the December days we spent trudging through fragrant Christmas tree lots to find the tree that was just right. Then we enjoyed pine scent in our house when the tree was finally placed in front of the window at home.

I suppose the tree became a fire hazard before Christmas was over. And I remember vacuuming pine needles off my shag carpet for weeks after the tree was removed, not to mention the shiny silver icicles that stuck to my socks.

Anyway, after years of enjoying genuine trees, we finally succumbed to a rather real looking fake one. But like I indicated, I not much of a fan for artificial trees. Still, they have some value at our age when you don't really want to go tripping through Christmas tree lots anymore.

First, they aren't lopsided. I never could find a real tree that didn't have a crooked limb. Fake ones look perfect, and they're clean and reusable - so we're saving our vacuum cleaner *and* the forests. But despite the benefits, I have already faced the ire of my kids who always appreciated a real tree.

My son, Jeremy, dropped by to eat some Christmas cookies which he knew were always available during the holidays. Looking over my shoulder with his hands on his hips, he scrutinized the store bought tree. "Mom, why did you, of all people, settled for a plastic tree?

I adjusted an ornament that he had made, long before he became so tall. "I was hoping you wouldn't notice," I said, "Besides, a real tree wouldn't fit in the car."

Jeremy carried on about it for a while. He teasingly said it was "Sacrilegious" to have a fake tree and it was almost as bad as a "fake Christmas." I knew exactly what he meant. He knows that I see the worst imitation ever as being a counterfeit Christmas. You know, that "Happy holidays" Christmas mentality that dares not mention Christ.

It's a counterfeit Christmas when we become too caught up in the outward things instead of the things of the heart. It's when we care more about the dead things than the living person. Are we more concerned about what kind of bag the groceries are put in rather than caring for the people standing beside us in the checkout line? A real Christmas is love when we keep Christ in **Christ**mas.

Of course you know the true meaning of Christmas doesn't really have anything to do with whether the tree is real. It goes infinitely beyond imitations and traditions.

A few weeks later, Jeremy stopped by the house after the festivities were over. I was getting ready to take down the tree and put it in the storage box.

Jeremy had to get in one last rub as he walked in the door and glanced at the fake tree. "It's not dead yet?"

I laughed at him. But his words provoked a good thought in my heart. All the imitations of the world will be gone someday, but Christ is forever.

Then the seventh angel blew his trumpet, and there were loud voices shouting in heaven: "The world has now become the Kingdom of our Lord and his Christ, and he will reign forever and ever." (Revelation 11:15 NLT)

45

Growing Old

It has been said that all men live lives of quiet desperation. Because of sin, mankind has suffered the curse of death (see Genesis 2:17), and that fact is ever before us. As the inevitable becomes closer, that desperation may intensify because of the cruel reflection in the mirror and the body that no longer cooperates. Then, people respond to growing old in different ways.

Some of us may attempt at restoring our youth to no avail; yet, we do many things. We may try products which claim to make one look young and conceal aging. Billion dollar industries provide makeup, creams, vitamins, energy drinks, hair restoration, wigs, implants, surgeries, Viagra, and so much more. Some exercise, diet, tan their bodies, go back to school, reinvest their money or relocate to another community, all in hope for refreshment.

People do a hundred things which will supposedly make them feel younger or lengthen survival. But there's no escaping the curse.

To add to the gloom, we see in this 21st century that our culture bestows eminence and superiority upon the young. In contrast, the elderly have been treated as if we are inferior. Evidence of this criteria can be seen on television, magazines and at the mall. Most things are geared to younger people, including styles, entertainment and advertisements. Even the church consider youth the most important attention.

In bygone years, seniors were respected and admired for their wisdom, but today we generally see a harsh outlook regarding the elderly and particularly, getting old. There's more than an implicit emphasis that aging is deplorable. (I have to admit, in some ways ... I have to agree, but the alternative of aging isn't very likeable either.)

The latter life process leading to the grave isn't easy. Eventually, there is a sort of settling in that is distinctive to the aged and that which youth resist. Nevertheless, submission is really not a choice. Nothing can be done to avoid the ending that all will face.

For some, the zeal for survival wanes early when they become passive, lose their appetites, no longer laugh or dance or love their life. That's not me, but, well ...there is provocation.

Who wants to remain in a world with poverty, immorality, crime, homosexuality, abortion, pornography, trafficking, adultery, thieves, murderers, starvation, sickness, fear and grief, just to mention a few things? There will be peace and joy and health with no tears in that glorious place where we'll be reunited with our loved one.

As we wait for that day, sometimes it helps to be around people who are near the same age, if there is opportunity to share one's interests, and perhaps feel less disregarded. There is something to be said for retirement homes. But I fear that some are merely a place of suffering with unity of complaints. Misery loves company they say. But it must not be that way.

So how does one face the twilight years optimistically? We may have become weary and are well spent, but God still supplies our need if we trust Him.

And my God shall supply all your need according to His riches in glory by Christ Jesus (Philippians 4:19 NKJV).

God gives joy and purpose. It's available for every human being at every age - and can still be chosen in our remaining years. In some cases, we have not because we ask not. Moreover, we mustn't stop working out our salvation just because we're old. (See Philippians 2:12.)

If there's a prescription to restore youth and health, it's having a thankful heart. Experts have researched and proved scientifically that there are health benefits in thankfulness, along with a distinct correlation between thanks giving and happiness. (I hope you test that statement for your own benefit.)

I've written to help identify some feelings about getting old. Our senior years are more opportunity for fulfillment and preparation for eternity. Don't refuse to talk about growing old, and particularly, death, as if somehow it could come sooner if it's discussed. I encourage you to examine your feelings and share them. And most importantly, be ready!

And as it is appointed for men to die once, but after this the judgment (Hebrews 9:27 NKJV).

This life is a less than a miniscule speck in eternity. Meanwhile, until that day, don't stop laughing, dancing and loving - because **you're only old once**!

END

Printed in Great Britain
by Amazon